THE BOOKENDS
OF THE CHRISTIAN LIFE

BOOK BY JERRY BRIDGES & BOB BEVINGTON

BIBLE STUDY LEADER'S GUIDE
BY SUSAN BEEBE

TABLE OF CONTENTS

Preface 3

Testimonies 5

Note to the Teacher 7

Introduction 9

The First Bookend: The Righteousness of Christ

    Chapter 1: The Righteousness of Christ 11

    Chapter 2: The Motivation of the Gospel 16

    Chapter 3: Gospel Enemy #1: Self-righteousness 23

    Chapter 4: Gospel Enemy #2: Persistent Guilt 29

    Chapter 5: Leaning on the First Bookend 36

The Second Bookend: The Power of the Holy Spirit

    Chapter 6: The Power of the Holy Spirit 43

    Chapter 7: Dependent Responsibility 50

    Chapter 8: The Help of the Divine Encourager 56

    Chapter 9: Gospel Enemy #3: Self-Reliance 62

    Chapter 10: Leaning on the Second Bookend 68

Conclusion: The Bookends Personal Worldview 74

Appendix 77

    Gospel Proclaiming Scripture Bookmark 75

    Song Lyrics 79

    Thomas Wilcox's Instructions for Dealing with Persistent Guilt 89

    A View of All Three Focal Points for Shifting Our Dependence to the Second Bookend 91

Bible Study Attached

Developed from *The Bookends of the Christian Life*, by Jerry Bridges and Bob Bevington, © 2009. Used by permission of Crossway, a publishing ministry of Good News Publishers, Wheaton, Illinois 60187, www.crossway.org.

PREFACE

The Bookends of the Christian Life, written by Bob Bevington and Jerry Bridges, has captivated many churches across the nation. The book has been used by God to transform the lives of many as it has provided a vehicle to "examine the framework that supports, stabilizes, and secures the believer's life in Christ."

The Bookends Bible Study and *Leader's Guide* were developed to give you the unique opportunity to dig even deeper into God's Word to explore the framework of God's plan of salvation and the Gospel. Learn how leaning on the Bookends of the Christian Life – the Righteousness of Christ and the Power of the Holy Spirit – can provide hope to live a life free from guilt, pride, and self-righteousness. Join us in exploring God's promises that will re-ignite your passion and appreciation for the gospel and motivate you to live a gospel-driven life.

TESTIMONIES

Testimony from using the Bookends Bible Study Guide for personal Bible study:

Kathy Ray Price MD:
Whether you are just starting your spiritual life "library" or have many volumes of study completed, *Bookends* is a study that will help your faith be clarified, strengthened, and deepened! I got so much more out of the book when I used the teacher's guide along with my study.

I wish I had known and trusted in the Biblical Bookend's principles my whole life! They really made the concepts of God's righteousness and the power of the Holy Spirit practical and applicable to every day life. I loved the scripture memory, deep study of scriptures, and songs that emphasized each lesson. Thank you for a study that helped add these critical "Bookends" to stabilize my Christian life on the bookshelf foundation of Christ!

Testimony from a small group leader who used Leader's Guide for their small group:

Our ladies' Bible study enjoyed the *Bookends* book, study questions, and awesome additional scriptures, explanations, and learning points from the teacher's guide! The ladies were from several denominations, various ages and walks of life, and yet all found applicable information for their faith growth.

Testimonies from those who participated in the Bookends Bible Study in a large group setting:

Kristen:
I think the study was great at really getting at the meat and potatoes of how to "use" the Bible or how to structure your life as a Christian.

Louisa:
In week one of Bookends, it was obvious our teachers had been impacted by the book. Their excitement and enthusiasm was contagious. I wanted to know what they had read and hear how God had impacted them. In this study, one of my favorite things was that each time we heard about an "ah ha" moment of someone's faith, it was linked to scripture and enabled me to have a deeper understanding of God's Word. While personal stories were shared, God's story was made clear and relevant for life today and communicated clearly. I don't think it would matter if I was a new believer or a believer for years, I would gain significantly from this study.

Jane:
Combining a visual image of two bookends with a practical understanding of the righteousness of Christ and the power of the Holy Spirit has transformed my life. The Scriptures have been unlocked for me. This knowledge often overflows into conversations with others. It provides a "nuts and bolts" working knowledge which gives me a newfound confidence to speak about God's love. Daily life makes much

more sense when I return to the concepts presented in *Bookends*. The book is concise, easy to read, and the Scripture references are well documented. It has become a terrific reference tool for me.

This *Bookends* study is multi-sensory and exciting to participate in. Information is presented passionately from the heart. Each study includes time for lecture, small group discussion, memory verses, and music. The variety of methods allowed me to connect through many facets in an intimate way. I am so grateful that the Holy Spirit led me to this study.

Christie:
Having just completed the *Bookends* Bible Study, I wanted to take a moment to recommend this study to anyone thinking of taking it. Whether you are new to faith in Christ or an "old timer" like my self (I've loved the Lord for over 50 years!) this study has something for you. The book itself is unique in its ability to clearly lay out the basics of the faith, and the study guide opens up excellent opportunities for class discussion. It is clear the writers have a passion for the Gospel. Churches should make this a regular in the rotation of Bible Studies they offer.

Judi:
Whether a new Christian or a mature believer, the *Bookends of the Christian Life* Bible study provides a unique opportunity to grow in one's faith. The study clearly and concisely portrays how the Righteousness of Christ and the Power of the Holy Spirit affect a believer's life. In the Gospel-driven life nothing happens randomly. Through the grace of Christ and the Power of the Holy Spirit we can be formed in the image He longs for us to be.

NOTE TO THE TEACHER

This Leader's Guide can be used in the following ways:

- As a large group didactic guide for the teacher in a Bible study setting
- As a small group leader's guide to emphasize learning points and clarify and amplify the material.
- As an individual study guide adjunct

Materials needed:

- *The Bookends of the Christian Life* by Bob Bevington and Jerry Bridges
- The Bookends Study Guide Questions *(included)*
- The Bookends Bible Study Leader's Guide *(included)*

Homework required: Read one chapter of *Bookends of the Christian Life* per week and complete corresponding Bookends Study Guide Questions. Answers to questions are addressed throughout teaching curriculum the following week.

Teaching format for a large group setting:

- The teaching curriculum is printed in outline format and is to be used as your guide.
- The time required to cover the teaching curriculum is approximately one hour per chapter. It is optimal to add an additional 20-30 minutes at the end of class to allow sufficient time for prayer and discussion.
- Each lesson follows the same basic format and includes the following:
    1. **Before you begin teaching:**
        - Write out the lesson's verses on the board ahead of time. The class can then record them before the study begins to better follow the lesson.
        - Pass out any materials needed such as song lyrics, bookmarks, etc.
    2. **Welcome and Prayer**
    3. **Quick Review** of previous week – includes reciting, as a class, the memory verse from the previous week
    4. **Teaching Content/Today's Lesson**
        - The teacher will speak most of the time, with periodic times of active dialogue in a question and answer format to avoid a "lecture" atmosphere. This teaching style keeps the students attentive while at the same time promoting class participation and a certain intimacy within the classroom.
        - Each lesson includes at least one **Break-Out Session** with designated Bible verses and corresponding questions to be discussed as a small group at each table, and then discussed

as a large group with the teacher after reconvening. This gives participants the opportunity to dig into God's Word together with a trained discussion leader.

- **Teacher's Notes** are added instructions on how to present material or conduct small group exercises.
- **Going Deeper** is an opportunity for the teacher to explore a topic more in-depth with students when time allows. This optional teaching material can be skipped if needed.
- The **Memory Verse** best summarizes the week's main teaching point and emphasizes the importance of scripture memory. The goal is to recite the verse as a class the following week.

5. The **Song of the Week**, played at the end of class, contains lyrics that summarize the week's teaching material.

6. **Small Group Discussion and Prayer Time** is an opportunity at the end of class for table leaders to review homework questions, collect prayer requests, and pray together.

   Suggestion: When time is limited, have participants summarize prayer requests to one sentence so that everyone's is heard, then if time allows, go back and discuss in more detail.

Recommended class structure in large group setting:

- The class should be divided into smaller groups that will stay at the same tables each week.
- Each table should have a leader who is a member of the church and has been trained to be a discussion leader.
- The table leader will be responsible for reviewing discussion guidelines with table members prior to discussion.
- Table leaders are responsible for preparing ahead of time for facilitating discussion and answering small group discussion questions during class. The discussion questions are added either at the end of class or will we built in throughout class time.
- The table leader will also be responsible for collecting prayer request and conducting prayer time at end of Bible study. This time is an important part of developing fellowship and intimacy within each small group.

Weekly Life Apps are additional resources that enable participants to "apply to their lives" what they are learning in the Bookends Bible Study. They include:

- **Memory Verse Booklets** – Provide small booklets for participants to record memory verses. Participants are encouraged to use the booklets for memorizing verses at home as well.
- **Song Lyrics** – Distribute lyrics (found in the Appendix) for the Song of the Week for participants to follow as they listen.
- **Prayer Requests Bookmarks** – Used as bookmark for the *Bookends* book, these are for each member to record weekly prayer requests. Every time the book is read, participants are reminded to pray for their group.
- **Small Group Discussion Questions** – Print these ahead of time for leaders to distribute for Breakout Sessions and Discussion Time.

INTRODUCTION
SESSION ONE

WELCOME and PRAYER

Introduce yourself and explain why you are excited about this study.

1. Share how God can use the concepts in this book to transform your faith and increase your appreciation for the Gospel.
2. This study can meet the needs of everyone in the class whether it's their first Bible study or they've been in Bible studies for years.
3. There is nothing more important than fully understanding the Gospel and what it means in our lives.

Discuss BUSINESS ITEMS and ANNOUNCEMENTS

Homework:

1. Weekly calendar/assignments
2. Read chapter and complete homework
    - Loose leaf paper should be in the back of the study for answers and notes.
    - Encourage students to try to finish all reading and questions but not to stress if they don't get it all done. Encourage them to please come regardless! This should be a low pressure Bible study.
3. Bring Bible!

Life Apps:

1. **Prayer Requests Bookmarks** – for each member at a table to record weekly prayer requests, these are used as bookmarks for *Bookends* book. Every time you pick up the book to read, pray for those in your group.
2. **Memory Verse Booklets**
3. **Breakout Sessions**
4. **Song Lyrics** – for Song of the Week

INTRODUCTIONS

Have each student say their name and why they are taking the study.

LEADER TESTIMONY

Explain how *Bookends* has transformed your faith.

BOOKENDS ILLUSTRATION

1. Ask participants to imagine all the activities (books) we balance in our lives. *(As they answer, label the books with their answers.)* Examples:

   - Christian Growth: church, Bible study, quiet time, serving, sharing the Gospel, fellowship
   - Everyday Activities/Necessities of Life: family activities, job, education, recreation, groceries, driving, laundry, cooking, household chores

2. The burden gets heavier and heavier and harder to manage as we add more activities. *(Give books to an assistant to hold. As the books get more difficult to manage, they will finally fall to the ground.)*

3. We need a bookshelf/solid foundation on which to place our books! **This solid foundation is found only in a relationship with Jesus Christ.** When we receive Christ as our Savior, we receive a great foundation (bookshelf) on which to place our books. *(Place books on a shelf.)*

4. Through this study, we will dive deep into God's Word to better understand the Gospel – no matter where we are in our walk, whether we've never picked up a Bible in our lives or we've been a Christian all of our lives. It's important to understand how desperately we need this foundation in our lives. Next week we will talk about the Gospel and why it provides such a solid foundation on which we can place our books.

5. Just because someone is a Christian doesn't mean life will be easy or without difficulty in managing activities. In other words…just because we have a nice bookshelf doesn't mean it's easy to manage the books. *(Start taking books off the shelf, then wobble the table. The books become unstable and fall.)*

> **TEACHER'S NOTE:**
> - You need a volunteer for this illustration.
> - Use 6-7 thick books wrapped in paper.

GOING A LITTLE DEEPER…

On top of the difficulty of trying to manage all our activities, we add a sense of guilt – guilt for what we should be doing or guilt for something we are doing that we shouldn't. We will read a whole chapter about guilt.

1. Guilt handled the right way leads us to change.
2. Guilt handled the wrong way…
   - Pharisees-focused on following the law and looking good on the outside, but were oblivious to the internal condition of their heart.
   - The guilt-riden are painfully aware of their sin and imperfections but keep trying harder and harder to become acceptable before God.

---

6. What would help? Two stable bookends can make all the difference in the world. **The two bookends are The Righteousness of Christ and The Power of the Holy Spirit.**

   - Through this study we are going to gain a better understanding and appreciation of the Gospel and the foundational truths that come from being united to Christ by faith.
   - We will learn how faith in Christ gives us access to the Righteousness of Christ and the Power of the Holy Spirit and the impact these two bookends can have on our lives.
   - We will answer questions that we often ask ourselves like… *(Read questions on page 16.)*

MEMORY VERSE

Galatians 5:1a – "It was for freedom that Christ sets us free, therefore keep standing firm…"

THE BOOKENDS OF THE CHRISTIAN LIFE — LEADER'S GUIDE

LEADER'S GUIDE CHAPTER ONE

FIRST BOOKEND: The Righteousness of Christ

WELCOME and PRAYER

1. Ask if everyone is enjoying the book so far.
2. How did the homework go?
3. As if anyone would be willing to share the memory verse from last week.

REVIEW

1. Last week we used books as representations of all the activities of our lives. *(Display books/bookends again.)*
2. We discovered that we need a good foundation/shelf (saving relationship with Christ) upon which to place our books.
3. Just because we have good foundation/relationship with Jesus Christ doesn't mean life is going to be easy.
4. We need to lean on the bookends of the Christian Life which are the Righteousness of Christ and the Power and the Holy Spirit.
5. We first need a bookshelf to place our books upon before we can rely on the bookends. There is nothing more important than understanding the Gospel that builds the foundation of our lives. This is the solid bookshelf.

> **TEACHER'S NOTE:**
> Before you begin:
> 1. Write verses on the board for class to look up ahead of time:
>   - Romans 3:23 and 2 Corinthians 5:21 in there entirety
>   - References to Matthew 22:30, Hebrews 12:14, Isaiah 59:2, 1 Peter 2:22, Hebrews 4:15, Matthew 11:27, Luke 3:23, Philippians 2:8, Colossians 1:22, Romans 5:21, Galatians 2:20
> 2. Select a few people to read verses out loud throughout teaching.
> 3. Pass Out Gospel Proclaiming Scripture Bookmarks
> 4. Song lyrics

LESSON ONE

What is the Gospel?

The Reality: We are all sinners, whether we like it or not. Romans 3:23 – "All have sinned and fall short of the glory of God."

> **TEACHER'S NOTE:**
> Have class members follow along with the Gospel Proclaiming Scripture Bookmark.

1. "All have sinned…" Why would some people question this?
   - "I am a pretty good person…I never killed anyone…I follow the ten commandments."
   - How about in our everyday lives? Unforgiveness, discontentment, selfishness, pride, judgementalism, jealousy, impatience, and irritability… The list goes on.
2. "…and fall short of the glory of God." What does God require of us? (Q #2)
   - Matthew 22:30 – "You shall love the Lord your God with all your heart, all your soul and all your mind."
   - 1 Peter 1:15-16 – "But he who called you is holy, you also be holy in all your conduct." Be holy in all our conduct?
   - Hebrews 12:14 – "Strive for…holiness without which no one will see the Lord."

3. Scripture says that righteousness (or holiness) is required in order to be in right standing with God. What is righteousness? (Q #1) Never doing what is wrong, always doing what is right, and perfectly obeying God.

The Problem:

1. There is no amount of good deeds that can restore our relationship with God. (Q #3)
    - Romans 3:10 – "None is righteous, no not one."
    - Isaiah 64:6 – "…all our righteous deeds are like a polluted garment (filthy rags)."
2. Refer back to Roman 3:23 – We "fall short of the glory of God."
    - What happens if we fall short of the glory of God? (Q #4)
    - Galatians 3:10 – "Cursed be everyone who does not abide by all things written in the Book of the Law and do them."
3. What does this curse means for us?
    - Isaiah 59:2 – "Your iniquities have made a separation between you and your God, and your sins have hidden his face from you so that he does not hear." We will be eternally separated from His presence.
    - Romans 6:23a – "For the wages of sin is death."

The Good News:

BREAK-OUT SESSION

1. Assign each table a verse to look up and read: Romans 6:23b, Galatians 3:13, 1 Peter 2:24, Romans 5:8, 1 Peter 3:18 *(Verses found on Gospel Proclaiming Scripture Bookmark)*
2. Discuss the following:
    - Who is the verse talking about?
    - Why is it Good News?
3. Have each table leader read verse out loud and give answers from the text they read.

> **TEACHER'S NOTE:**
> Table leaders should remind group members of discussion guidelines.
> Have everyone at the table introduce themselves.

PULL IT ALL TOGETHER

Summarize class input to answer questions:

1. Romans 6:23b – "BUT the gift of God is eternal life in Christ Jesus our Lord." God gives us eternal life through Christ!
2. Galatians 3:13 – "Christ redeemed us from the curse of the law by becoming a curse for us."
    - Remember the curse? What are the wages (payment) of sin? DEATH! (See Romans 6:23a)
    - Christ redeemed us from the curse that ultimately leads to death and eternal separation from God.

3. 1 Peter 2:24 – "He bore our sin in His body on the tree." He paid the price for our sins by sacrificing His body. (Q #6)

4. Romans 5:8 – "But God demonstrates his own love for us in this: while we were still sinners, Christ died for us."

    - When did God demonstrate His love for us? While we were still sinners!
    - Did He die because I was a good person? NO! He died because I was a sinner.

5. 1 Peter 3:18 – "For Christ also suffered once for sins, the righteous (Christ) for the unrighteous (us)."

MEMORY VERSE

2 Corinthians 5:21 – "For our sake he made him to be sin (put on our filthy rags), who knew no sin, so that in him we might become the righteousness of God."

THE COATS ILLUSTRATION

Imagine a Moral Ledger recording all of our good deeds and all our sins.

TEACHER'S NOTE:
1. You will need:
    - Two volunteers
    - One dirty coat and one "sparkly white coat"
2. Write ledger on board:

US		CHRIST	
Sins	Good Deeds	Sins	Good Deeds

1. Our Moral Ledger
    - Sin – We are completely sinful. Romans 3:23 – "For all have sinned…"
    - Good Deeds – Even our most righteous deeds are like filthy rags (Isaiah 64:6). They are nothing compared to the righteousness of Christ! *(Have a volunteer put on the filthy rag coat.)*

2. Christ's Moral Ledger
    - Sin – He "knew no sin" (2 Corinthians 5:21) (Q #6). "He committed no sin" (1 Peter 2:22). Jesus was "in every respect tempted as we are, yet without sin" (Hebrews 4:15).
    - Good Deeds? – He is perfectly righteous *(Have another volunteer put on the sparkly white coat.)*
    - He was in perfect relationship with His Father. What does that mean? Matthew 11:27 says, "No one knows the Son except the Father, and no one knows the Father except the Son and anyone to whom the Son chooses to reveal to Him." It is an exclusive relationship with intimate knowledge of each other.
    - He was perfectly obedient. The Father takes delight in all His Son does. When Jesus was baptized, God said, "You are my beloved Son, with you I am well pleased" (Luke 3:23).

    The epitome of Christ's obedience was when He humbled Himself by becoming obedient to the point of death, even death on a cross (Philippians 2:8).

THE GREAT EXCHANGE

1. When Christ died, He became sin. 2 Corinthians 5:21 – "For our sake he made him to be sin…"
    - He put on our filthy sin coat.
    - God took our sins and charged them to Christ leaving us with a clean ledger!

2. 2 Corinthians 5:21 – "…So that in him we might become the righteousness of God."

    Isaiah 61:10 – "…for he has clothed me with the garments of salvation and he has covered me with the robe of righteousness"! (Q #6) *(Have the volunteers exchange the filthy sin coat for the "sparkly white coat.")*

3. From the moment we receive Christ as our Savior and put our faith in what He did for us on the cross, God no longer sees our sin, but sees Christ's righteousness!

    - This makes us acceptable to stand before our Holy God. Discuss Colossians 1:22 – "He has now reconciled in his body of flesh by his death, in order to present you holy and blameless and above reproach before him."
    - Quote from Pastor Joe Coffey: "Christ lived the life that we should have lived and died the death that we should have died."
    - Just as God charged our sin to Christ, He credits the perfect obedience of Jesus to all who trust in him.

Why does the Great Exchange bring us Good News?

1. We now can enjoy an intimate relationship with God because the wages of our sin have been paid!

    - God's gift of His Son, Christ, paid the penalty for our sins! So just as God charged our sin to Christ, He credits the perfect obedience of Jesus to all who trust in Him. Christ lived a perfect life-in God's sight it is *as if* we lived a perfect life.
    - This not only gives us eternal life in the presence of our Holy God, but we can have the awesome joy of having a relationship with Him in our daily lives!
    - How can I be sure God loves and accepts me? (p. 16) Because when He looks at me He sees His Son and loves and accepts me as His Son.

2. The Good News of the Resurrection

    - After Christ died, He rose again! (Ephesians 4) He did not stay full of sin. Instead, He rose from the grave, conquered sin and death and regained His righteousness.
    - Because of His resurrection, we as believers do not have to remain under the dominion of sin and death. (Romans 6:14) That is the joy behind the resurrection.

3. Because of His death and resurrection we are justified. Romans 4:25 – "He was delivered over to death for our sins and was raised to life for our justification."

    - What does justification mean? Two ways of looking at it: (Q #7)

    1) "Just as if I'd never sinned" refers to the transfer of our moral debt to Christ so we are left with a "clean" ledger – also known as forgiveness. Our sins have been wiped clean.

    2) "Just as if I'd always obeyed" refers to our slate that in now filled with the very righteousness of Christ. Because we are clothed in His righteousness (Isaiah 61:10).

    - How are we justified? Romans 5:1 – "…we have been justified <u>by faith</u>" (Q #6) When we put our <u>faith</u> in Christ's death and resurrection, we are justified.
    - When are we declared justified? The moment we genuinely trust in Christ as our Savior, we are declared righteous by God. This is a one-time event.

How do we apply this Good News to our lives?

1. Read Galatians 2:20a – "I have been crucified with Christ. It is no longer I who live, but Christ who lives in me..."

    - Christ died on the cross to pay for our sins.
    - When we receive Christ, we become crucified with Him, die to our own life, and have freedom to live a new life in Christ.

2. Read further in Galatians 2:20b – "And the life I live in the flesh I live by faith in the Son of God, who love me and gave himself for me"

    - "I live" Justification is not only a past event, but also a daily present reality. Every day, Paul realized he stood righteous in the sight of God.
    - "by faith..." Faith involves a renunciation and a reliance. (Q #8; page 28)

      Renunciation – We must renounce any trust in our own performance as the basis of our acceptance before God.

      Reliance – We must rely solely on Christ's perfect obedience and His sin-bearing death as the sole basis of our standing before God

3. "Every day we must re-acknowledge the fact that there's nothing we can do to make ourselves either more acceptable to God or less acceptable." (Q #9; page 29) We must look outside ourselves daily to the righteousness of Christ.

SONG

"In Christ Alone" by Owl City ("Here in the Power of Christ I'll Stand")

INVITATION

If anyone here has never placed their faith in what Christ did for them and would like to talk more about having a personal relationship with Christ, please let one of us know. We would love to talk with you more.

DISCUSSION TIME

1. Table leaders should have small groups share prayer requests.

2. Discussion Questions:

    - As believers who are justified by faith, why do we fall back into relying on our own performances?
    - How can we start to live this out in our daily lives?

TEACHER'S NOTE:
Print discussion questions ahead of time or write them on the board.

LEADER'S GUIDE CHAPTER TWO

The Motivation of the Gospel

WELCOME and PRAYER

> **TEACHER'S NOTE:**
>
> Before you begin:
>
> 1. Write verses on the board for class to look up ahead of time: Isaiah 6:1-8, Luke 7:36-50, Acts 9:1-9, Romans 6:1, Romans 12:1, Ephesians 2:8, Philippians 3:4-14
> 2. Select a few people to read verses out loud throughout teaching.
> 3. Song lyrics

REVIEW

Memory Verse: 2 Corinthians 5:21 – "For our sake he made him to be sin who knew no sin, so that in him we might become the righteousness of God."

1. When we put our faith in the redeeming work of Christ's death on the cross, we are clothed in the **Righteousness of Christ**.

2. When God looks at us, He sees His Son. Because of that, we can have a relationship with Him. We are no longer separated from Him.

3. Does He love us because of anything we have done? No!

Ephesians 2:8 – "For by grace you have been saved through faith. And this is not your own doing; it is the gift of God, not a result of works, so that no one may boast." This brings up some good questions:

1. If we are saved by grace and there is nothing we can do to earn our salvation, why would we be motivated to serve?

2. If our sins are already paid for by Christ's blood, why can't we just go on sinning?

3. Look to scripture for more insight...

    - Romans 6:1 – "What shall we say then? Are we to continue in sin that grace may abound? By no means!"

    - Romans 6:12-13 – "Let not sin therefore reign in your mortal body, to make you obey its passions. Do not present your members to sin as instruments for unrighteousness, but present yourselves to God as those who have been brought from death to life." Where does the motivation to serve and "present yourself to God" come from?

LESSON TWO
The Motivation of the Gospel

Three-Step Process

A genuine love for Christ and the motivation to serve Him come through this three-step process: (Write these on board.)

1. An on-going consciousness of our own sinfulness and unworthiness (Q #2)

2. The assurance of forgiveness that only comes from the power of the Gospel (Q #2)

3. When we have experienced the transforming power of the Gospel, we respond with genuine gratitude and a commitment to God through the power of the Holy Spirit.

BREAK-OUT SESSION

Explore the following three people from the Bible and how each experienced the transforming power of the Gospel. Then discuss what this looks like in our own lives.

1. Sinful Woman - Luke 7:36-50 (Q #1)
2. Highly Respected Jew – Isaiah 6:1-8 (Q #4-5)
3. Self-Righteous Pharisee – Philippians 3:4-14 (Q #8-9)

> **TEACHER'S NOTE:**
>
> Before you begin:
>
> 1. Have each table look up and read designated passages.
> 2. Have them focus on designated questions from the homework relating to the passage.
> 3. Reconvene and discuss stories as a class.

PULL IT ALL TOGETHER

As each story is discussed have a representative from each table discuss their answers related to their designated scripture.

The Sinful Woman – Luke 7:36-50

1. Who invited Jesus into his home? (vs. 36)

    Simon, the Pharisee (a very elite group of Jews who followed the law – very religious)

2. Who is also there? (vs. 37-38)

    The "woman of the city." It was unusual for someone with a bad reputation to dare enter uninvited into the house of a Pharisee.

3. What did the sinful woman do when she heard Jesus was there?

    - Brought an alabastar flask of ointment – very expensive
    - Stood behind Him at His feet – guests were reclined at the table
    - Wept and wet His feet with her tears – out of thankfulness and reverent awe
    - Washed His feet – an act of hospitality
    - Wiped His feet with her hair – had to loosen her long hair which Jewish women rarely did in public
    - Kissed His feet and anointed them with her expensive ointment – a huge sacrife
    - Why would she do this? It was an outward symbol of her heartfelt gratitude and affection towards Jesus.

3. Why is Simon the Pharisee upset? (vs. 39 – Q #1a) If Jesus was a prophet, He would have known the woman touching Him was a sinner.

4. How does Jesus respond?

    - He told the parable of the money lender and two debtors. One owed 500 denarii and the other owed 50. When they couldn't pay, he cancelled the debt of them both.
    - He asked a question – Which of them loved the money-lender more? Simon answered that it was the one whose larger debt was cancelled. Jesus said that was correct because the money-lender whose larger debt was cancelled had more to be thankful for, therefore loved more.

5. How does Jesus use the parable to make His point? (vs. 44-50)

    - He compared this story with the love reaction of the sinful woman and Simon's reaction to Jesus. The sinful woman knew she was a forgiven sinner and showed great gratitude through her actions. Simon had no water for His feet, no kiss, no anointing with oil – no response of gratitude.

    - There is a profound difference between the way Simon and the woman treated Jesus. What does this tell us about how they viewed their sinfulness? (Q #1b) The woman recognized her sins and her need for forgiveness much more than Simon.

6. What is Jesus' point in telling this story? (vs. 47)

    - Simon sensed no need for forgiveness, so he showed little love for Jesus.

    - The woman sensed Jesus' forgiveness, therefore, she loved much.

    - It is important to note that the woman wasn't forgiven because she loved much, but rather, she loved much because she was forgiven.

> **TEACHER'S NOTE:**
> Be prepared for tough questions like: "What if we feel there is little for which we need to be forgiven? Does that mean we lack appreciation and therefor love little?"

7. Jesus said to the woman, "Your sins are forgiven." (verse 48) Why did Jesus say this after her outward display of affection? He wanted to make her forgiveness public, especially the forgiveness of a well-known sinner in front of Simon and his guests.

How do we see the Three-Step Process in this woman's experience?

1. How can we tell she was conscious of her own sin?
    - She was obviously deeply convicted for her sins *(from initial encounter with Jesus)*.
    - She was seeking forgiveness.
    - She entered into a pharisee's house to seek-out Jesus.

2. How is she assured that she is forgiven? (verse 48) She received assurance from Jesus that her sins were forgiven.

3. What was her response of love and gratitude? (Q #3) She wet and washed Jesus' feet with her tears and anointed Him with expensive ointment.

The Highly Respected Jew – Isaiah 6:1-8

The Background of Isaiah

> **TEACHER'S NOTE:**
> Explain that sometimes we have to read a little before and after a passage to fully grasp the context of the story.

1. We don't know much about Isaiah. What we do know:

    - Isaiah was a member of a royal family. He was the son of Amoz, therefore his uncle was Amaziah, King of Judah.

    - Isaiah is a book of vision focused on the character and promises of God.

    - Judah had moved from dependence on God's power towards unbelief and judgment.

2. The first five chapters of Isaiah focuses on Jerusalem and Judah. In chapter six, he shifts his focus to himself as he describes a vision he had of the Lord.

> **GOING A LITTLE DEEPER...**
>
> They were putting their hope in pagan powers and false teaching. Isaiah 3:8 says, "For Jerusalem has stumbled and Judah has fallen, because their speech and deeds are against the Lord."
>
> The message of Isaiah: Although the Lord brings judgement, there is hope for redemption.

The Text – Isaiah 6:1-8

Isaiah 6:1-3

1. When is this happening? (vs. 1) King Uzziah had just died, "marking the end of an era of national prosperity."

2. Who does he see and where is he seated? (vs. 1) The Lord sitting upon a "throne, high and lifted up; and the train of his robe filled the temple..." This suggests the Lord's Majesty.

3. He describes a seraphim (fiery angelic being) (vs. 2). Why do you think he covered his face and feet with his wings? This indicates that even a superhuman creature humbles himself before a holy God.

4. "Holy, Holy, Holy is the Lord of hosts; the whole earth is full of his glory." (vs. 3) This describes God's infinite holiness.

Isaiah 6:4-5 – "Woe is me! For I am lost; for I am a man of unclean lips..."

1. How does Isaiah respond to seeing the Lord? How does he view himself in light of being in the presence of a Holy God? (Q #4)

2. Why do you think he had this kind of response?
   - Becoming more aware of God's holiness made him more aware of his own sinfulness.
   - The more we get to know God the more we see our own sin!

3. Why is this surprising considering Isaiah was very religious and highly respected?
   - He was doing all the right things but understood that "even his most righteous deeds were like filthy rags"! – Isaiah 64:6
   - His situation was the total opposite from the sinful woman in Luke 7 because she was a known sinner.
   - Even though outwardly he seemed righteous, Isaiah considered himself just as sinful as the woman in light of God's holiness. (Q #6)

4. We are all in the same boat!

> **TEACHER'S NOTE:**
> Use the story of Jonah as an analogy. Jonah was highly religious and the sailors were clearly sinners, yet they were all sinners – all in the same boat!

Isaiah 6:6-7

1. As Isaiah was recognizing his sinfulness, the seraphim touched his mouth and said, "Behold… Your guilt is taken away, and your sin atoned for."

2. Just like the sinful woman in Luke 7, Isaiah had a deep conviction of his own sinfulness and experienced the assurance of God's forgiveness. (Q #6)

Isaiah 6:8

1. The Lord says "Whom shall I send, and who will go for us?"

2. How does Isaiah respond? "Here am I! Send me!"

3. Why do you think he responded this way?

    - He responded by offering himself to God out of deep gratitude.

    - Both the woman and Isaiah, when in the presence of a Holy God recognized the deep gulf between His holiness and their sinfulness.

    - When we have experienced the transforming power of the Gospel, we respond with genuine gratitude and commitment to God. (Q #6)

Isaiah experienced the same Three-Step Process (Q #6)

- Acute realization of his own sinfulness in light of God's holiness

- Hearing the Gospel that his sins were forgiven

- Response of gratitude, love, and surrender of his life

The Self-Righteous Pharisee

The Background of Paul

Before the Gospel – Philippians 3:4-6

1. Before the Gospel, Paul had every reason to be confident in the flesh. He was…

    - Circumcised on the eighth day

    - Of the people of Israel, tribe of Benjamin, Hebrews of Hebrews – belonged to a long line of Jewish ancestry

    - A Pharisee – consumed with following the law but did not accept Jesus' resurrection or the Gospel

    - Zealous – but for the wrong thing. He persecuted the church. Paul thought he was defending the holiness of God. He did not believe Jesus was the Son of God.

2. According to verse 6, if Paul's righteousness was based on following the law, what would he be considered? (Q #8a) "As to righteousness under the law – blameless."

Paul's Conversion – Acts 9:1-9

> **TEACHER'S NOTE:**
> It is important to briefly review how Paul became a believer so you are able to show the impact the Gospel had on him.

1. "Saul, still breathing threats and murder against the disciples of the Lord." (vs. 1)

2. He was traveling to Damascus to arrest Christians when a light from heaven flashed around him. (vs. 2-3)

4. He fell to the ground and heard a voice, saying "Saul, Saul, why are you persecuting me?" Saul said, "Who are you Lord?" The Lord replied, "I am Jesus, whom you are persecuting. But rise and enter the city, and you will be told what you are to do." (vs. 4-6)

5. He was blinded for three days and was led into Damascus by those traveling with him. Ananias was called by the Lord to lay hands on Saul so he could regain his sight and "be filled with the Holy Spirit." (vs. 7-17)

6. "…Immediately something like scales fell from his eyes, regained his sight, he rose and was baptized… Immediately he proclaimed Jesus in the synagogues saying, 'He is the Son of God.'" (v. 18-20) Why immediately? He was grateful for his salvation and wanted to respond in gratitude.

After Paul's Conversion – Philippians 3:2-14

1. Refer back to Philippians 3:7-9. "Whatever gain I had, I counted as loss for the sake of Christ… Not having a righteous of my own that comes from the law, but that which comes through faith in Christ, the righteousness from God that depends on faith."

2. According to verses 7-9, where does Paul realize his righteousness comes from? (Q #8b) He understands that his own righteousness is not a means of attaining a right standing with God. It is only by the shed blood and righteousness of Christ.

3. What was Paul's reaction to the Gospel? Refer back to Acts 9:20. "Immediately he proclaimed Jesus in the synagogues saying, 'He is the Son of God'"

4. Paul renounced his own righteousness and relied solely on the righteousness of Christ. How did that fuel his desire to pursue Christ-likeness and serve God whole-heartedly? (Q #9) Philippians 3:14 – "I press on toward the goal for the prize of the upward call of God in Christ Jesus." His "zeal" was no longer motivated by a desire to earn God's favor but by love and gratitude for the righteousness of Christ that was given to him by faith.

Summary of Paul's Testimony

Just like the sinful woman and Isaiah, after life-changing experiences with the Gospel they were then highly motivated by gratitude to love, worship and serve God.

The Application

A genuine love for Christ comes through…

1. First Step – An on-going consciousness of our own sinfulness and unworthiness:

   - We all fall somewhere on the spectrum between the sinful woman, Isaiah, and the Pharisee. Where are you on the spectrum?

   - We are all in the same boat! We all need to experience the same three-step process. For some, the steps come suddenly and dramatically. Others experience them more gradually.

   - Regardless of where we are on the spectrum, we need to recognize that we need a Savior.

2. Second Step: The assurance that no matter how great or small our sins, they have been forgiven through His death on the cross
3. Third Step: When we experience the Gospel, it motivates us to lay down our lives out of pure gratitude.

    Our Goal: We need to intentionally bath our minds and hearts in the gospel every day!
    - "Preach the gospel to ourselves daily!!" – Jerry Bridges
    - Remind ourselves of what He did to redeem us of our sin and give us eternal life.
4. The Results:
    - Increased awareness of God's holiness as we get to know Him more
    - Increased awareness of our own sinfulness
    - A deeper understanding of the meaning and application of the Gospel
    - A response of genuine gratitude and experience of the motivating power of the Gospel

What does this response of genuine gratitude look like in our lives?

1. **MEMORY VERSE:** Colossians 2:6-7 – "Therefore, as you received Christ Jesus the Lord, so walk in him, rooted and built up in him and established in the faith, just as you were taught, abounding in thanksgiving."
2. As we have received this awesome gift of salvation, how are we to respond? What does it look like to walk in Him?
3. Romans 12:1 says, "I appeal to you therefore, by the mercies of God, to present your bodies as a living sacrifice, holy and acceptable to God, which is your spiritual worship." (Q#10) What is the "therefore" there for? In Romans, Paul spent the previous 11 chapters teaching about the Gospel. In light of everything he as just said, Paul "appeals" to us to respond to the Gospel by presenting our bodies as a living sacrifice to God.

SONG

"Motion of Mercy" by Francesca Battistelli

DISCUSSION TIME

1. According to Colossians 2:6-7, we are to "walk in Christ." What does that look like?
2. Romans 12:1 says, "I appeal to you, therefore, by the mercies of God, to present your bodies as a living sacrifice…
    - What does it mean to present your bodies as a living sacrifice? Page 39 in the book refers to "the entirety of our lives offered continuously to God!"
    - Do we really offer ourselves as a living sacrifice daily? What if we have been a Christian for many years, or we've done a million Bible studies and grew up in the church? Is it more of a duty than a joyous response to the Gospel?

LEADER'S GUIDE CHAPTER THREE

GOSPEL ENEMY #1: Self-Righteousness

WELCOME and PRAYER

REVIEW

> **TEACHER'S NOTE:**
> Before you begin:
> 1. Write verses on board for class to look up: Genesis 15:6; Acts 13:32; Romans 4:13; Galatians 1:6-8, 2:16, 2:21, 3:13-14; Philippians 3:9; Hebrews 10:10; 1 Peter 1:18-19
> 2. Song Lyrics

1. Genuine love for Christ and the motivation to serve Him come through:
   - An on-going consciousness of our own sinfulness and unworthiness
   - The assurance of forgiveness that only comes from the transforming power of the Gospel
   - When we have experienced the power of the Gospel, we respond with genuine gratitude and commitment to God.

2. With gratitude and commitment, we are to "walk in Him" and "present ourselves as a living sacrifice."
   - MEMORY VERSE: Colossians 2:6-7 – "Therefore, as you received Christ Jesus the Lord, so walk in Him, rooted and built up in Him and established in the faith, just as you were taught, abounding in thanksgiving."
   - Romans 12:1 – "I appeal to you therefore, by the mercies of God, to present your bodies as a living sacrifice, holy and acceptable to God, which is your spiritual worship."

Two Enemies of the Gospel

When we rely on our own performance instead of the righteousness of Christ for salvation, two things can occur:

1. **Self-righteousness** – We respond to the Gospel by resting in the assurance that we are a good person – "good enough" to earn God's love
2. **Persistent Guilt** – We respond to the Gospel with anxiety over the inadequacy of our performance and not being good enough or "worthy" of His love.

In both cases we rely on our own righteousness, not on the righteousness of Christ.

Gospel Enemy #1 – Self Righteousness

1. What is self-righteousness? (Q #1)
   - We think of "snobs, conceited, holier-than-thou people." These words are usually used when describing human relationships.
   - What kind of self-righteousness are we dealing with when it comes to the Gospel? (Q #2) Self-righteousness towards God.

2. What does self-righteousness look like? Typical answers to the question, "If you died today and God asked you why he should let you into heaven?" would be: "I'm a pretty good person…I go to church every Sunday…I go to Bible Study every week…"

3. On what are these people dependent? (Q #6) Their own works and their own righteousness.

How does the Gospel change everything?

We go back to the Great Exchange. 2 Corinthians 5:21 – "For our sake he made him to be sin who knew no sin, so that in him we might become the righteousness of God."

1. What makes us acceptable before God?

    - When Christ died, He paid the price for our sins by becoming sin for us.

    - In turn, He clothed us with the righteousness of Christ.

    - When God looks at us He sees Christ – not because of anything we have done, but because of what Christ did for us!

2. When we place our faith in the Gospel, this not only allows us to have eternal life with Him, but enables us to have a daily personal relationship with Him and receive the many blessings that come when we receive Christ as our Savior.

   TEACHER'S NOTE:
   Further discussion: Six "A"mazing Blessings of God on page 42 – a great list of blessings from receiving Christ as Savior and a relationship with Him

3. When we depend on our own performance to justify our standing before God, we are being self-righteous (as if we deserve it) (Q #3), which defeats the whole purpose of Christ dying on the cross.

    - Galatians 2:21 – "I do not nullify the grace of God, for if righteousness were through law (our own performances), then Christ died for no purpose." Anytime we are self-righteous, we are totally disregarding what Christ did for us.

    - If we could be righteous (in right standing with God) by our actions, then Christ's death meant nothing!

BREAK-OUT SESSION

Galatians – An example of self-righteousness

Background on the Book of Galatians

TEACHER'S NOTE:
Have each table read Galatians 1:6-8 and discuss the answers to question 4 from this week's homework before discussing the Case Study as a class.

1. Galatians was written by Paul to the churches of Galatia. He helped establish these churches during his first missionary journey after his conversion (Acts 9). After his conversion, he immediately started proclaiming Jesus' name.

2. What was Paul's purpose for writing the book of Galatians?

   Galatians 1:6-8 – "I am astonished that you are so quickly deserting Him who called you in the grace of Christ and are turning to a different gospel – not that there is another one, but there are some who trouble you and want to distort the Gospel of Christ. But even if we or an angel from heaven should preach to you a gospel contrary to the one we preached to you, let him be accursed."

3. Why was Paul astonished with the Galatians? (Q #4a)

- They were already "quickly" deserting Him (Christ). Remember, it was a short amount of time between the time that he had preached the Gospel to them and they were quickly deserting Him!

- They were "turning to a different gospel." What does that mean? (Q #4b)

    …Putting your hope in anything besides the hope that Christ gives.

    …When "someone proclaims another Jesus than the one we proclaim…accept a gospel different than the one you accepted." (2 Corinthians 11:4)

    …"A man-centered, performance-based, legalistic approach to making oneself acceptable before God." (p. 44)

4. What was different about this gospel the Galatians were turning to? It is important to understand the true Gospel that Paul preached before one can discern this different gospel. The beauty of God's Word is that the Gospel is interwoven throughout, originating in the Old Testament. For this lesson, we are taking a necessary trip back to the Old Testament to discover where God's promises originated and how the Gospel unfolds with the fulfillment of those promises through Christ.

True Gospel

Paul preached the TRUE Gospel found in God's Word. He proclaimed that Jesus was the Son of God (Acts 9:20), "the Christ" (Acts 9:22), the promised Savior (Acts 13:32).

> **TEACHER'S NOTE:**
> Refer to the beginning of Paul's ministry, immediately after his conversion in Acts 9 and 13.

The Promise: Acts 13:32 – "We bring you good news that what God promised to the fathers, this he has fulfilled to us their children by raising Jesus."

1. To whom is this promise? **"To the fathers"** is referring to Abraham. In the Old Testament, God established a covenant with Abraham. Genesis 17:7 says, "I will establish my covenant between me and you and your offspring." This promise was made not only to Abraham, but his descendants as well. We will discover later that we are a part of his offspring through faith.

2. What kind of promise was this?

    - It was a **covenant promise** made by God. A covenant is an agreement – a promise to keep your promise.

    - It was a **promise of blessing**. Genesis 12:3 – "And in you all the families would be blessed." This included promises of descendants and land. (see Genesis 15)

    - It was an **everlasting promise**. Genesis 17:7-9 – "Throughout generations for an everlasting covenant."

> **GOING A LITTLE DEEPER…**
> For further study, see Romans 9:4 for the promised blessings to the Israelites: Adoption, Glory, Covenants (promies to save them), Law, Worship, Promies. (Reference: ESV Study Bible)

3. What were Abraham and his descendants to do as sign of the covenant? Circumcision - Circumcision of the flesh was a sign of the covenant between God and the Israelites and was done to distinguish those who believed in God's promises. This was a part of the Law. (Genesis 17:1-14)

4. How did Abraham respond to the covenant God made with him?

- Genesis 15:6 – "Abraham believed God and it was counted to him as righteousness." God counted Abraham righteous because he believed God would keep His promises. (Romans 4:3)
- It is important to note that Abraham was counted righteous before he was circumcised. (Romans 4:9-12) He was considered righteous by God before he could prove himself righteous by his deeds (obedience).
- Why? Because of his faith!

5. So, "…the promise to Abraham and his offspring that he would be heir of the world did not come through the law, but through the righteousness of faith." (Romans 4:13)

    > **TEACHER'S NOTE:**
    > Later we will learn the answer to: "If our righteous-ness comes through faith and not the Law, why do we need to obey?"

    - Abraham would receive the blessings not because of his deeds or because he was circumcised, but because of his faith.
    - Through this faith, he stood righteous.

6. How did God ultimately fulfill His promise? Through Christ's death and resurrection! Acts 13:32 – "By raising Jesus." This was the True Gospel!

Different Gospel

In what false gospel were the Galatians putting their hope? A false gospel that the Judaizers were teaching.

1. Background: The Judaizers were false teachers from Jerusalem who preached a gospel of grace *plus* works to the Gentiles. After Christ's death and resurrection, some conservative Jewish Christians argued that in addition to the work of Christ's death on the cross, the Gentiles should live by the Jewish ceremonial laws (like circumcision and dietary laws) as a means of justification before God.

2. Why the law?
    - In the Old Testament, God gave the Israelites the Law because of their perpetual sin and complaining. He gave them the Law to point out to them their sin.
    - The Law required obedience. The Israelites would receive blessing for their obedience and a curse for their disobedience. (See Deuteronomy 11:26-28) Remember Galatians 3:10 – "<u>Cursed</u> be everyone who does not abide by <u>all things</u> written in the Book of the Law and do them."
    - The Jews made blood sacrifices for their sin (referred to as an atonement) at the Tabernacle because according to the Law, "Without shedding of blood there is no forgiveness of sins." (Leviticus 5:11, 17:11; Hebrews 9:22) It had to be the blood of a perfect animal. They thought that the blood of the animals would pay for their sins. The high priest would carry animal blood into the Most Holy Place on the annual Jewish Day of Atonement to make a sacrifice for the forgiveness of sin. (Exodus 30:33, Leviticus 4:14, 20)
    - Therefore, it was very difficult for these Jews, having heard the Good News of Christ, to forsake the traditions handed down from their forefathers. Following the Jewish ceremonial laws became their way of life – making themselves acceptable before God.
    - This is why the Jewish leaders were having a hard time understanding the idea of being justified only by their faith.

3. Back to the Galatians

- The Judiazers were trying to convince the Galatians to add back certain customs ("works of the law") to make them acceptable before God.
- The Judiazers were teaching them that "Unless you are circumcised according to the custom of Moses, you cannot be saved." (Acts 15:1)
- Why circumcision? According to the Old Testament, one had to be circumcised to belong to the people of God. (Genesis 17:10) There was even a debate between Paul and Peter over this. (Galatians 2:12)

4. What was this different Gospel? The Galatians were deserting the true Gospel that Paul preached and falling back into relying on their own human effort (obeying the Law) to be justified by God.

Paul was writing to the Galatians to remind them of the good news of Christ.

Galatians 3:13-14 – "Christ redeemed us from the curse of the law by becoming a curse for us...*so that* in Christ Jesus the blessing of Abraham might come to the Gentiles, *so that* we might receive the promised Spirit through faith."

1. What did Christ do? Christ redeemed us from the curse by becoming a curse for us!

2. Why did He do this?
    - *So that* in Christ Jesus the blessing of Abraham (being justified by faith) might come to the Gentiles. Good news is that through faith in Christ the blessings have come to us, as Gentiles.

> **GOING A LITTLE DEEPER...**
> In Isaiah, there is prophecy that this blessing would come to the Gentiles. Originally, the promise was only for the Jews... but because of Christ... we as Gentiles are part of His family.

- *So that* we might receive the promised Spirit through faith. This is talking about the Holy Spirit. (We will talk about this in the second half of the study.)

3. So what is the True Gospel that Paul preached?
    - Paul was telling the Galatians that they would receive the blessings of standing righteous by God (the inheritance of eternal life and forgiveness of sins) through faith in Christ.
    - The promise was fulfilled by Christ's death on the cross.

How does the True Gospel defeat the enemy of self-righteousness?

Galatians 2:16 – "A man is not justified by the works of the Law but through faith in Christ Jesus, even we have believed in Christ Jesus, so that we may be justified by faith in Christ and not by the works of the Law."

1. How are we justified? "Through faith!" (Q #5a)

2. What about the Galatians' works and following the Law?
    - Galatians 2:16 – "Not by works." (Q #5b)

- Peter 1:18-19 – "You were ransomed from the futile ways inherited from your forefathers, not with perishable things such as silver or gold, but with the precious blood of Christ, like that of a lamb without blemish or spot." This is why He is referred to as the "Lamb of God." He was the "Lamb" without blemish or spot to be the perfect sacrifice. The shed blood of the perfect "Lamb of God" gains us forgiveness of our sins and reconciliation with our God.
- What about circumcision? Galatians 5:6 – "For in Christ Jesus neither circumcision nor uncircumcision means anything, but faith working through love."

GOING A LITTLE DEEPER...
See Romans 2:29 – "Circumcision is a matter of the heart."

- Hebrews 10:10 – "We have been sanctified through the offering of the body of Christ once and for all."

3. Christ was our perfect sacrifice. The blood sacrifices seen throughout the Old Testament were foreshadowing of the true, once and for all sacrifice of Christ. He was our atonement – our sin offering.

MEMORY VERSE

Philippians 3:9 – "and may be found in Him, not having a righteousness of my own derived from the Law, but that which is through faith in Christ, the righteousness which comes from God on the basis of faith."

How does this relate to us?

1. What about our sacrifices and good deeds? We are made righteous by what Christ did for us on the cross – not by anything we have done. We are justified by our faith in what He did for us.
2. Just like the Galatians, anytime we rely on our own performance as a means of being acceptable before God or to earn our salvation, we are being self-righteous.

SONG

"On Christ the Solid Rock I Stand" by Avalon

DISCUSSION TIME

1. Read and discuss Luke 18:9-14 (The Pharisee and a tax collector praying in the temple) for another example in the Bible of self-righteousness. (Q #9)

    How do we know that the Pharisee was dependent on his own righteousness? "God, I thank you that I am not like other men...adulterers...I fast twice a week...I tithe..." He assumed his standing before God was secure based on his obedience compared to others and his lack of scandalous sins. Anything on our spiritual resume is like "filthy rags" to Christ. No amount of personal performance will ever gain the approval from a holy God.

2. Look at the questions on page 49 of your book. Can you identify with some examples of how we can be self-righteous in our everyday lives? (Q #10)

THE BOOKENDS OF THE CHRISTIAN LIFE   LEADER'S GUIDE

LEADER'S GUIDE CHAPTER FOUR

GOSPEL ENEMY #2: Persistent Guilt

> **TEACHER'S NOTE:**
> Before you begin:
> 1. Write verses on board for class to look up: Genesis 3:1-13; Ezekial 18:30b; Psalms 139:24; Romans 2:14-15, 8:1; Galatians 2:21; Colossians 1:13; 1 Timothy 1:13-14; Hebrews 9:14; 1 John 2:12
> 2. Song Lyrics

WELCOME and PRAYER

REVIEW

1. Two Categories of Self-righteous Believers

   - First Category (Chapter 3) – We respond to the Gospel by resting in the assurance that we are good people – "good enough" to earn God's love. Faith and confidence are based on our own performance or our lack of scandalous sins.

   - Second Category (Chapter 4) – Persistent Guilt – We partially embrace the Gospel but constantly live under a sense of guilt. We know we are falling short of the expectations we set on ourselves and assume God is displeased as well.

2. The Problem with Self-righteousness

   - We rely on our own performance as a means of being justified before God and earn our salvation.

   - We are not relying on the first bookend – the Righteousness of Christ.

3. Galatians Case Study – A great example of self-righteousness in the Bible

   - The Galatians were deserting the True Gospel for a different gospel, putting their hope in their own obedience of the Law to obtain the blessing of being righteous before God.

   - Any time we put our hope in our own performance or something other than the righteousness of Christ, we are putting our trust in a different gospel.

4. The True Gospel

   - Defeats the enemy of self-righteousness when we solely put our hope in what Christ did for us to make us righteous before our Holy God.

   - Galatians 3:13-14 – "Christ redeemed us from the curse of the law by becoming a curse for us…"

5. MEMORY VERSE: Philippians 3:9 – "And may be found in Him, not having a righteousness of my own derived from the law, but that which is through faith in Christ, the righteousness which comes from God on the basis of faith." We need to remind ourselves of the Gospel everyday! There is nothing we could ever do or not do to change God's love for us.

LESSON FOUR

Gospel Enemy #2: Persistent Guilt

What is guilt? "An awareness of having done wrong…accompanied by feelings of shame and regret." *(The Encarta dictionary FamilyLife.com)*

What kinds of things do we feel guilty about? (Could be little or big)

1. Things we *should* be doing, but are not – sins of omission (reading the Bible more, praying more, reading to our kids)
2. Things that we *shouldn't* be doing, but are – sins of commission (drinking too much caffeine, gossip, long list!)

What about guilt that is not justified or healthy?

1. Feeling guilty about things that are not necessarily bad. (Example: Spending a lot of time at church) or feeling guilty about something that is not necessarily your fault (Example: poor choices of your wayward child.)
2. Why do you think you are feeling guilty for those things? Examine your own heart. Is what you are doing in line with God's will? Are you doing it for the right reasons? If what you have done is not in line with God's will, then it should lead you back to the cross.

When Christians fail to deal properly with guilt, we can fall into a pattern of **Persistent Guilt.** We fall into a feeling of condemnation –aware of our sin but intentionally or unintentionally avoiding the solution, which is the Gospel.

What happens when we suffer from persistent guilt?

1. When we sin, we feel guilty not only because we have fallen short of our own expectations, but we feel that we have fallen short of God's expectations as well.

    - We all fall short! Remember what we learned about the Gospel the first week? Romans 3:23 – "All have sinned and fall short of the glory of God." We have all fallen short of God's perfect standard!
    - But the Gospel changes things. Romans 5:8 – "But God demonstrates his own love for us in this: while we were still sinners, Christ died for us." Because of what Christ did for us on the cross, our sins have been paid for, and it is His righteousness that we are clothed in that makes us acceptable before God.
    - When we wallow in persistent guilt, we lean on our own performance (or lack thereof) to make us acceptable before God – instead of on the righteousness of Christ. In a way, this is a form of self-righteousness. (Q #1)

2. Persistent guilt also implies that not only do we fall short, but Christ's death for us also fell short of its intended purpose.

    - The purpose of the cross was to erase all our guilt and sin so we could stand righteous before our Holy God. When we wallow in our guilt we are saying that Christ's death was not enough – insufficient. We are neglecting the True Gospel!
    - That's why Paul was saying to the Galatians "I do not nullify the grace of God, for if righteousness were through law, then Christ died for no purpose" (Galatians 2:21). We must remember that Christ died and paid the price for our sins so we don't have to wallow in persistent guilt!

Dealing with the stronghold of guilt goes all the way back to the Garden of Eden.

BREAK-OUT SESSION

The First Experience of Guilt in the Bible

Genesis 3:1-13 – "…the serpent was more crafty…he said to the woman "Did God actually say, You shall not eat of any tree in the garden?"… The woman said "We may eat fruit…but not of the tree in the midst of the garden…lest you die."

> **TEACHER'S NOTE:**
> Have small groups read Genesis 3:1-13 from homework question #2. Then reconvend and discuss the following questions in italics.

1. *Who is in this story?* Adam, Eve, and the serpent (Fallen Angel, "Lucifer," – Isaiah 14:12-13)

2. *What did the serpent tell Adam and Eve?* The serpent said (v. 4-5), "You will not surely die. God knows that when you eat of it your eyes will be opened, and you will be like God, knowing good and evil." Is this the truth or a lie? Perhaps a false gospel?

3. *What happens next?* "She took of its fruit and ate, she also gave some to her husband and he ate" (v. 6). She believed another gospel…and gave in to the temptation.

4. *What happens immediately after Adam and Eve ate the fruit?* "Then the eyes of both were opened and they knew they were naked…sewed fig leaves together and made loin clothes" (v. 7).

5. *What do you think it means that, "Their eyes were opened"?* (Q #2) They thought it would help them be like God. Instead, their eyes were opened to their sin.

6. *Why did they sew fig leaves?* They realized they were naked when their eyes were opened to their sin, and they felt guilty.

> **GOING A LITTLE DEEPER…**
> God provided a covering (garmet) for Adam and Eve in v. 21. First evidence in the Bible of God making a sacrifice of an animal (shed blood) so that they could be "covered."

7. What did Adam and Eve do when they heard the Lord walking in the garden? How did they respond to their guilt? "They heard the sound of the Lord God walking in the garden…the man and his wife hid themselves from the presence of the Lord" (v. 8). When you find yourself hiding, ask why. You know what you are doing is wrong and you feel guilty!

8. How did Adam respond to the guilt? He blamed it on Eve (v. 12). Eve blamed it on the serpent. How often do we blame our sin on someone else? "I sinned because she made me angry" Who did the sinning? Remember Ephesians 4:26 – "Do not sin in your anger."

9. How did Adam and Eve know they had done wrong? God gave them a conscience.

What is a Conscience? (Q #3)

1. What do we know about the conscience?

    - It is the "instinctive sense of right and wrong that produces guilt when violated." (Bible Commentary definition)

    - Every human has a conscience, whether he or she is a Christian or not. It can be influenced by many things – media, upbringing, God's Word, etc.

2. What does the Bible say about the conscience?

- Gentiles have a conscience. Romans 2:14-15 – "For when Gentiles, who do not have the law, by nature do what the law requires, they are a law to themselves, even though they do not have the law. They show that the work of the law is written on their hearts, while their conscience also bears witness."
- It is evident that that God gave the Galatians a conscience — even though the Gentile believers were free from the law, they showed that the law was still "written on their hearts."

3. It is important to note that our human conscience is not always a perfect moral guide.

- The Galatians struggled with "conflicting thoughts" about their moral behavior that would either "accuse or even excuse them" (Romans 2:15).
- As a believer, God gave us the Holy Spirit to remind us of His Word and help us discern our conscience and determine right from wrong. (Q#3) See John 14:26.

TEACHER'S NOTE: We will address the role of the Holy Spirit in more detail later in the book.

What did God design the conscience to do for us? (Q #3b)

1. It sends off a warning signal when we are about to go astray. Did Eve listen to the warning signal? Genesis 3:2 – "We may eat fruit…but not of the tree in the midst of the garden." No, she went ahead and sinned.

2. When we sin, our conscience declares us guilty. How did Eve respond to the guilt? She hid from God.

When we neglect our conscience, we can begin to engage in destructive behaviors.

Ineffective ways of handling a guilty conscience (Q #4):

1. **Use escape mechanisms** – turn to other things like TV, movies, sports, hobbies, even drug or alcohol abuse. These numb the pain of our conscience and temporarily make us feel better about ourselves, possibly leading into deeper sin.

2. **Rationalize and create double standards** – "Well at least I don't do…", "I don't have any other vices, so this is my only vice…"

3. **Hide the problem** – not seek help and try to fix it first before facing Christian friends.

4. **Use non-biblical concepts to cope** – "You must learn to forgive yourself." (Q #9)

5. **Ignore the nagging and become numb to it** – Repeatedly rejecting your conscience can eventually incapacitate you (Q #7). 1 Timothy 1:19 – "By rejecting [the conscience], some have made shipwreck of their faith."

TEACHER'S NOTE: What is wrong with this thinking? We do not have the authority to forgive ourselves. Only God can do that. This could potentially lead to delicate subject matter that may be better discussed in a small group setting.

What is wrong with all of these coping strategies? What is the danger? (Q #6)

1. The message of the cross is absent when your guilt is handled ineffectively. It can lead you further away from the gospel and neglect the God-given purpose of the conscience!

2. A conscience without the Gospel only leads to more guilt and feelings of condemnation.

Only the life and death of Christ can break you free from a guilty conscience.

MEMORY VERSE

Hebrews 9:14 – "How much more will the blood of Christ, who through the eternal Spirit offered himself without blemish to God, purify our conscience from dead works to serve the living God." Hebrews 9:14

1. Christ was our perfect sacrifice, the perfect Lamb of God, without blemish – John 1:29 (Remember Chapter 3)
2. What purifies our conscience? (Q #10) When He sacrificed His body and shed His blood, our sins were paid for, our slates were wiped clean – giving us a purified conscience to start new and serve our God!

How do you move from the grip of persistent guilt to healthy conviction that leads us to the Gospel?

Guilt-Conviction-Gospel-Repentance

1. **Guilt**
   - Unhealthy guilt ignores the cross. Adam and Eve hid from God.
   - Acknowledging your sin and feeling remorseful is healthy when it leads you to the Gospel!
2. **Conviction** – A healthy remembrance of our sin is a blessing (Q #12).
   - The more we are in God's Word, the more convicted we become as the Holy Spirit reminds us of our sin.
   - You can ask God to reveal your sin to you, as in Psalm 139:5 – "See if there is any offensive way in me."
   - Evidence of healthy conviction in Paul's life is found in 1 Timothy 1:13-14 – "Formerly I was a blasphemer, persecutor..." Paul recognized his sin, but he didn't stay there. He did not stay in a state of self-condemnation.
3. **Gospel**
   - The Gospel changed Paul! See the rest of 1 Timothy 1:13-14 – "But I received mercy... and the grace of our Lord overflowed for me ... Christ Jesus came into the world to save sinners of whom I am the foremost." Convicted of his sin, Paul went straight to the cross.
   - Healthy conviction drives us to the cross.. Don't wallow in guilt and self-condemnation! Take it to the cross and leave it there. Remember, you have been forgiven. Remember why Christ died!

     ...1 John 2:12 – "Your sins are forgiven for his name's sake"

     ...Romans 8:1 – There is, therefore, now no condemnation for those who are in Christ Jesus!

     ...Colossians 1:13 – "He has delivered us from the domain of darkness and transferred us to the kingdom of his beloved Son, in whom we have redemption and forgiveness!"
4. **Repentance**
   - Once we have acknowledged our sin, we must move to reentance.

- The Biblical translation definition: is "a change of mind about sin and about God, which results in turning from sin to God."

- Turn away from your sin and repent/make right.

    …Ezekiel 18:30b – "Repent and turn from all your transgressions."

    …Corinthians 7:10 – "For godly grief produces a repentance that leads us to salvation without regret, whereas worldly grief produces death."

- This may be a lot easier said than done. We could be talking about habitual sin we have been dealing with for years. It's only by the power of the Cross that we can turn away from sin to live new life.

GOING A LITTLE DEEPER…

For in-depth study, see Wilcox's instructions. It may be helpful to print for participants for Discussion Time at the end of class or for personal study.

Wilcox's Instructions

Puritan Thomas Wilcox described six ways to deal with persistent guilt by shifting our focus. (Q #13)

1. Shift your focus away from your sin and onto Christ. Don't wallow in your guilt! Take it to the cross and leave it there.

2. Shift your focus to Christ our mediator. Hebrews 9:15 – "Therefore, he is the mediator of a new covenant, so that those who are called may receive that promised eternal inheritance…"

3. Shift your focus to Christ crucified, risen, and ascended. Mark 16:5-6 – "Jesus was crucified and risen."

4. Shift your focus to the glory of Christ. Colossians 3:1 – "If then you have been raised with Christ, seek the things that are above, where Christ is, seated at the right hand of God. Set your minds on things that are above, not on things that are on earth."

5. Shift your focus off of self-condemnation. Romans 8: – "There is therefore now no condemnation for those who are in Christ Jesus."

6. Shift your focus off self-contempt. Remember, Paul did not wallow in his self-contempt. Paul says, "But I received mercy… and the grace of our Lord overflowed for me" (1 Timothey 1:13-14).

SONG

"Not Guilty" by Mandisa

SUMMARY

- The only way to escape the grip of guilt is to run to the Gospel! It's OK to remember your sin, but don't stay there! Let guilt remind you of the Gospel!

- Remember: Guilt–Conviction–Gospel–Repentence. We have already been delivered. His stripes have already healed you! (Colossians 1:13-15, Isaiah 53:5)

- When we do this, persistent guilt can be transformed into joyful gratitude for the Gospel!

DISCUSSION TIME

1. Read the ten questions on page 56 and answer question #8 and #14 in the Study Guide.

2. Puritan Thomas Wilcox described six ways to deal with persistent guilt by shifting our focus. Which of these do you find helpful and why? (Q #13)

LEADER'S GUIDE CHAPTER FIVE

Leaning on the First Bookend

WELCOME and PRAYER

> **TEACHER'S NOTE:**
> Before you begin:
> 1. Write verses on the board for class to look up: Psalm 139:24, Luke 19:1-10, Galatians 3:7
> 2. Song Lyrics

REVIEW

1. Because of what Christ did for us on the cross, we have the Righteousness of Christ as a bookend on which to lean our books.

   - There is nothing we can say or do that would make us righteous before God. It is what Christ has done for us that makes us clothed in the righteousness of Christ, so we can stand acceptable before our Holy God.

   - When God looks at us, He sees Christ's righteousness and can look at us with love. Do we truly feel this way day to day?

2. As we discussed in Chapters 3 and 4, we tend to lean on our own righteousness to give us confidence and hope. This leads to **Self-Righteousness and Persistent Guilt**.

   - Any time we rely on anything but the righteousness of Christ to gain the acceptance of a Holy God, we are being self-righteous.

   - Wallowing in persistent guilt is ultimately being self-righteous instead of relying on Christ's death as payment for our sins. It neglects the very purpose of the cross. We need to use our guilty conscience and conviction to lead us to the cross instead.

3. Guilt-Conviction-Gospel-Repentance

   - We need to remember what Christ did for us, instead of wallowing in our guilt.

   - Let the Gospel remind us that we are forgiven and our sins have already been paid for by Christ's blood! And then turn away from that sin.

4. MEMORY VERSE: Hebrews 9:14 – "How much more will the blood of Christ, who through the eternal Spirit offered himself without blemish to God, purify our conscience from dead works to serve the living God."

5. Only the life and death of Christ can break us free from persistent guilt. We need to recognize our self-righteousness and shift our dependence back on to the first bookend – the Righteousness of Christ.

Growing in the Gospel: A Diagram

The diagram below is based on a timeline that starts with your physical birth. It tracks two "awarenesses:"

1. Your awareness of God's holiness
2. Your awareness of your own sinfulness

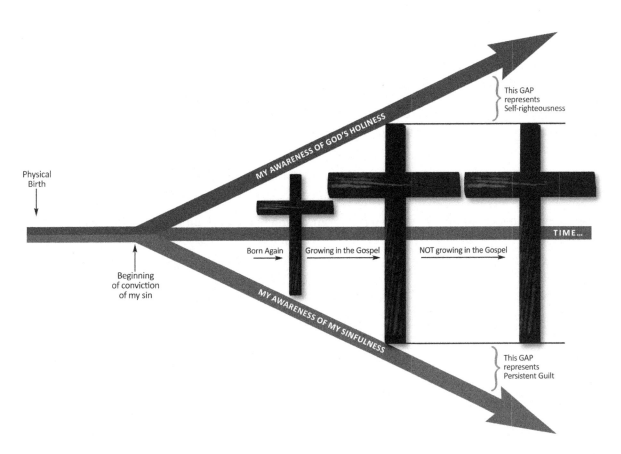

At first, you are aware of neither. But at some point, due to the work of the Holy Spirit convicting you of "sin, righteousness, and judgment" (see John 16:8), you begin to become painfully aware of both. As this process continues and the message of Good News is revealed—faith is awakened and you become born again.

However, as time goes on, you become increasingly aware:

1. God is even more holy than you previously realized
2. We are even more sinful than you previously realized

This is where your awareness of the extent of the grace of the Gospel <u>must</u> also increase. This is illustrated by the cross in the diagram becoming bigger—meaning that no matter how holy you realize God is, and no matter how sinful you realize you are, the righteousness of Christ is always all-sufficient for you.

As you begin to realize God is even more holy than we knew before, if you fail to grow in the Gospel, a gap will form at the top. Gospel Enemy #1 will appear as you attempt to fill this gap with your own righteousness, as if to say, "I will provide my own righteousness because, as great as Christ's righteousness is, it is not quite enough for the likes of me."

Likewise, as you begin to realize that you are even more sinful than you knew before, if you fail to grow in the Gospel, a gap will form at the bottom. Gospel Enemy #2 will appear as you attempt to fill this gap with persistent guilt, as if to say, "I will bear my own guilt because, as great as Christ's guilt-bearing is, it is not quite enough for the likes of me."

LESSON FIVE

Leaning on the First Bookend

1. Although this chapter is called "Leaning on the First Bookend," a more appropriate word to use is dependence. What does it mean to "lean" on the First Bookend? (Q #1) Dependence on the first bookend means "relying on, trusting in, and placing our confidence, faith, and hope in the righteousness of Christ" (p. 66).

2. What do we depend on to give us value? What is the object of our dependence? Do we really depend fully on the righteousness of Christ to make us acceptable before God?

3. There are **three focal points that help us shift our dependence back on to the Righteousness of Christ** (Q #3) Much of this has to do with our level of appreciation of the Gospel.

    - Seeing ourselves as **desperately lost sinners**
    - Seeing the **righteousness of Christ** as all-sufficient for us daily
    - Seeing and **rejecting our functional saviors**

BREAK-OUT SESSION

TEACHER'S NOTE: Have small groups read the story aloud then discuss question #5 from homework.

A Case Study of Zacchaeus – Luke 19:1-10

1. Who was Zacchaeus? The chief tax collector and a rich man who had taken everyone's money.

2. What was he doing? He was trying to see Jesus, but couldn't.

3. Why? He was too short.

4. How did he see Jesus? He climbed a sycamore tree.

5. What happened next? As Jesus was passing by, He looked up, told Zacchaeus to come down out of the tree, and invited himself to Zacchaeus' house.

6. How did Zacchaeus react? (Q #5a) He hurried down and received Him joyfully.

7. How did the crowd react? They grumbled because Jesus was going to be the guest of tax collectors who were generally dishonest and despised by everyone.

8. Why would this make them grumble? The Pharisees thought that if someone had fellowship with a sinner, it would make them unclean.

9. What was Zacchaeus' next response? He called Jesus "Lord" and immediately gave half of his goods to the poor and restored "fourfold" everything to anyone he had defrauded.

10. What was Jesus' response? Jesus declared that Zacchaeus was saved and a true son of Abraham. Zacchaeus received the inheritance that only Jesus can bring. "For the Son of Man came to seek and to save the lost."

Focal Point #1: Seeing ourselves as desperately lost sinners

1. How do you think Zacchaeus was able to see himself as a desperately lost sinner?

TEACHER'S NOTE: Discuss how the three focal points helped Zacchaeus shift his dependence back on to the Righteousness of Christ.

- Being in the presence of Jesus caused Zacchaeus to recognize that he was lost and in need of a Savior. (Q #5b-c)
- A similar reaction came from the tax collector in Luke 18:13 (Chapter 4). The self-righteous Pharisee was thanking God that he was not like other sinners and bragged of his righteous deeds. But the tax collector, known for being despised and dishonest, recognized his sinfulness and begged for God's mercy.

2. Why is it sometimes difficult for us to see ourselves as desperately lost sinners?
    - We say things like: "I'm a good person. I go to church every Sunday, I volunteer, I follow the Ten Commandments." We compare ourselves to "more sinful" people, thinking our sins are not "that bad."
    - We may not yet have been convicted of a certain sin. In these cases, we have not come to the realization that what we are doing grieves Him.
    - Looking at the list on p. 68 reminds us that we are "desperately lost sinners!" (Q #8) A sin is a sin is a sin. "All have sinned and fall short of the glory of God." Remember from Lesson 2: We're all in the same boat!

3. What helped Zacchaeus recognize his sinfulness?
    - Being in the presence of Jesus. The closer we get to the light, the more sin is exposed. (Q #7).
    - Psalm 36:9 – "For with you is the fountain of life; in your light do we see light."

4. How can we recognize our own depravity?
    - Just like Zacchaeus – being in the presence of the Lord. Spending time in God's Word to know Him more.
    - When standing in the presence of a Holy God, our own righteousness becomes nothing more than filthy rags. We recognize that no matter how "good" we may be, it is totally inadequate before God.

5. What if you have a hard time understanding or admitting your depravity? Genuinely ask God to open the eyes of your heart. Pray scripture:
    - Ephesians 1:18 – "…having the eyes of your hearts enlightened, that you may know what is the hope to which He has called you, what are the riches of His glorious inheritance in the saints." When we "see with the eyes of our heart" the amazing blessings we have in Christ, we become aware of how undeserving we are of them. (Q #4)
    - Psalm 139:24 – "See if there is any offensive way in me." Our true depravity will be exposed in the light of his holiness.

6. What do we do once we recognize our own depravity?

    We shift dependence from our own goodness back to the one thing that can bring us into relationship with God – the righteousness of Christ given to us by God's amazing grace.

Focal Point #2: Seeing the Righteousness of Christ as all-sufficient for us daily

1. How does Zacchaeus see the Righteousness of Christ as all-sufficient?

- In verse 9, Jesus said, "Today salvation has come to this house, since he is also a son of Abraham. For the Son of Man came to seek and save the lost."
- Why was he a son of Abraham? He may have technically been an offspring of Abraham because he was a Jew. But in this case why was he a son of Abraham? Because of his heritage or his wealth? No! It is because of his faith.
- Galatians 3:7 – "It is those of faith who are the sons of Abraham" (Chapter 3). Acts 13:32 – "We bring you good news that what God promised to the fathers, this He has fulfilled to us their children by raising Jesus." Genesis 15:6 – "Abraham believed God and it was counted to him as righteousness."
- We, too, get the promise of being declared righteous before God because of our faith in what Christ did for us!

2. Zacchaeus saw that he was not saved because of the amount of possessions he had or his heritage. Despite his sinfulness, the Righteousness of Christ was all-sufficient for him to be accepted. It was all that was needed for him to be saved.

3. How can we be reminded of the sufficient Righteousness of Christ?
    - **Remind ourselves that Jesus was perfectly obedient as our substitute** – in every area of our lives (Q #9). In areas where we see failure and sin, Jesus provides a perfect obedience that is credited to us. Example: If we lack patience, Jesus was patient in our place (p. 70). (Q #10) What are you lacking? Christ lived the life that we should have lived!
    - **Preach the Gospel to ourselves everyday.** (Q #11) First thing in the morning, praise God for what He did for you. Confess your sins. Thank Him for dying the death that you should have died and living the life you should have lived so that you can stand righteous before God and have a relationship with Him.
    - **Mediate on God's promises** from the Gospel in light of our sins. (Example p. 71)

4. What is the benefit of being reminded of the Righteousness of Christ? It reminds us that:
    - We see ourselves as desperately lost sinners.
    - We've been rescued by the all-sufficient Righteousness of Christ.
    - Increases our appreciation for the Gospel daily.

Focal Point #3: Seeing and Rejecting our Functional Saviors

1. **What is a functional savior?**
    - Something we depend on other than the Righteousness of Christ to satisfy, fulfill, or "save" us – anything we embrace that isn't God.
    - Functional saviors can become our source of identity, security, and significance. They preoccupy our minds and consume our time and resources. Functional saviors make us feel good and sometimes righteous. For example, parenting, serving in the church, etc.

2. **Why are functional saviors enemies of the Gospel?** (Q #12)
    - They make us turn away from the Gospel.

- Depending on functional saviors for hope is idolatry. Exodus 20:3 – "You shall have no other gods before me." Functional saviors control us and we worship them.

3. **What was Zacchaeus' functional savior?** Money, he would do anything to get it. His self-worth depended on his wealth.

4. **What did Zacchaeus do with his functional savior?** When Zacchaeus met Christ, he saw that his functional savior was totally insufficient and dramatically shifted his dependence on to the Righteousness of Christ.

5. **What are we to do with our functional saviors?** (Q #13)
    - Identify them. They can be people, things, or activities. They can be harmful to our bodies like drugs, alcohol, overeating, lack of eating. Or they can seem harmless, even good, like family, friends, TV, sleep, caffeine, careers, hobbies, sports, relationships, possessions, a clean house, exercise, even ministry. See fill in the blank survey p. 73.
    - Reject them! Once we have identified a functional savior, reject it by turning our focus back on to the only source of hope.

6. **Biblical example of functional savior:** God used the prophet Jeremiah to warn Judah against functional saviors.
    - Jeremiah 2:11-13 – "My people have changed their glory for that which does not profit… Be appalled… be shocked… for my people have committed two evils: they have forsaken me, the fountain of living waters, and hewed (chop with an ax) our cisterns (tanks of water) for themselves, broken cisterns that can hold no water." ("Hewed cisterns" lead to broken cisterns which cannot hold water because they leak.)
    - Functional saviors cannot be depended upon! They leak, they leave us thirsty!
    - Depending on a functional savior requires us to forsake God. No wonder Jeremiah finds this "appalling and shocking!" (v. 12)

7. **What happens when we don't reject our functional saviors?**
    - We end up leaning on our functional savior instead of the first bookend. Functional saviors are unreliable. If we trust in bookends that are un-sturdy, they won't hold us up and we will fall!
    - God knows our heart and when we fall into dependence on functional saviors. Sometimes He "mercifully intervenes. As a surgeon skillfully removes a cancerous tumor before it kills, so our master physician will cut way our sinful attachments." (p. 74)
    - How does God "mercifully intervene"? In the form of testing and trials – increased physical disabilities, disappointments in work, being defrauded in a business transaction. He may even use mundane experiences – a flat tire or lost luggage. We eventually realize the things of this world cannot give us eternal security, identity, or worth.

8. **What are we to do with these functional saviors?**
    - We are to identify them, then remove or reject them.
    - Shift our dependence back to the living God, the fountain of living waters that will never run dry.
    - Depend on the lasting righteousness that saves, fulfills, and sustains us forever.

MEMORY VERSE

"But lay up for yourselves treasures in heaven, where neither moth nor rust destroys and where thieves do not break in and steal. For where your treasure is, there your heart will be also." Matthew 6:20-21 (ESV)

SONG

"Grace" by Laura Story

DISCUSSION TIME

1. Where is your treasure? In what are you putting your hope?
2. Look at the fill-in-the-blank exercise on p. 73. Which one do you identify with the most? (Q #13)
   - Once we have identified our functional savior(s), what are we to do with them? What can happen when we don't reject our functional saviors?
   - Currently, what is God doing in your life to help free you from your functional saviors?

THE BOOKENDS OF THE CHRISTIAN LIFE

LEADER'S GUIDE CHAPTER SIX

THE SECOND BOOKEND: The Power of the Holy Spirit

WELCOME and PRAYER

REVIEW Chapters 1-5

> **TEACHER'S NOTE:**
> Before you begin:
> 1. Write verses on the board for class to look up: John 14:16; Romans 8:11; 2 Corinthians 3:18; Ephesians 1:13-14, 3:16; Philippians 2:13-14; 2 Timothy 2:1; Hebrews 13:20-21
> 2. Song Lyrics

1. Three focal points that help shift our dependence back on to the Righteousness of Christ:

    - Seeing ourselves as desperately lost sinners
    - Seeing the righteousness of Christ as all-sufficient for us daily
    - Seeing and rejecting our functional saviors

2. We learned how important it is to shift our focus…

    - Off of ourselves or anything we look towards to give us worth (functional saviors)
    - Back on the Righteousness of Christ

3. MEMORY VERSE: Matthew 6:20-21 (ESV) – "But lay up for yourselves treasures in heaven, where neither moth nor rust destroys and where thieves do not break in and steal. For where your treasure is, there your heart will be also."

    - Where is your treasure? Where do you put your hope? Is it in the everlasting Righteousness of Christ? Or is it in the things of this world that won't last forever?
    - As our understanding and appreciation for the Gospel grows, our motivation to rely on the first bookend (the Righteousness of Christ) also grows.
    - We need more than just the motivation to rely on the Righteousness of Christ. We need the Power of the Holy Spirit!

LESSON 6: The Power of the Holy Spirit

Who is the Holy Spirit? He is a member of the Trinity – Father, Son, and Holy Spirit

> **GOING A LITTLE DEEPER…**
> For further study of the Trinity, refer to Ephesians 3:14-17 – a great representation of the three parts of the Trinity.

Why did God give us the Holy Spirit?

1. Before Jesus was crucified, He explained to His disciples that even though He would no longer be with them on earth, He would send a "Helper" that would be with them forever.

    - John 14:16 – "And I will ask the Father, and He will give you another Helper, to be with you forever."
    - John 14:26 – "But the Helper, the Holy Spirit, whom the Father will send in my name, He will teach you all things and bring to remembrance all that I have said to you.

2. Does this promise only apply to the disciples? No! Romans 8:14 – "For all who are led by the Spirit of God are sons of God." This promise of the Holy Spirit applies to all believers. God sent the Holy Spirit to indwell in all that are sons of God through faith.

How do we gain access to the Holy Spirit?

Ephesians 1:13-14 – "In Him you also, when you heard the word of truth, the Gospel of your salvation, and believed in Him, were sealed with the promised Holy Spirit, who is the guarantee of our inheritance until we acquire possession of it…"

1. When do we receive the Holy Spirit? When we hear the Word of Truth, the Gospel of Salvation, and believe in Him.

2. What happens when we hear and believe?

    - "We are sealed with the promised Holy Spirit."

    - What does it mean to be sealed? (Q #2) Definition: a mark of ownership often used by ancient kings to signify ownership. The ESV Study Bible notes in 2 Corinthians 1:21-22 that when we receive the Holy Spirit, it certifies the authenticity of our acceptance by God as being genuine. (ESV Notes)

3. How is the Holy Spirit a "guarantee?"

    - Definition of "guarantee"– a financial term referring to the first installation paid as a pledge of faithfulness to complete a purchase. (On-line dictionary)

    - The Holy Spirit is God's pledge to complete His final redemption of His people when Christ returns. The Holy Spirit protects and preserves Christians until they reach their eternal inheritance.

4. When we understand the true Gospel and the implications of what Christ did for us, and we receive Him as our personal Savior, we receive the Holy Spirit.

Why do we need the Power of the Holy Spirit?

The reasons we need the Power of the Holy Spirit are endless.

1. **To help us in times of trouble (Helper)**

    - John 14:16 – "…He will give you another Helper."

    - Why do we need a Helper? John 16:33 – "I have told you these things, so that in me you may have peace. In this world you will have trouble. But take heart! I have overcome the world."

    - What will we have in this world? Trouble (ESV version says "tribulation")

    - What is "tribulation?" Definition – "grievous trouble; severe trial or suffering."

    - What other kind of tribulation? Ephesians 6:12 – "For we do not wrestle against flesh and blood, but against the rulers, against the authorities, against the cosmic powers over this present darkness, against the spiritual forces of evil in the heavenly places."

    - What do we wrestle with? "Rulers, authorities, cosmic powers…spiritual forces of evil"

- What does the rest of John 16:33 say? "Take heart, I have overcome the world!" When Christ died on the cross, death was defeated and these "spiritual fores of evil" were put to shame. Colossians 2:15 – "He disrmed the rulers and authorities and put them to open shame by triumphing over them in Him." The Holy Spirit living inside of us is greater than any evil we face.

> **GOING A LITTLE DEEPER...**
> For further study on how Jesus has "overcome the world," see:
> - Ephesians 1:21 – "He is "far above all rule and authority and power and dominion."
> - 1 John 4:4b – "For He who is in you is greater than he who is in the world."
> - 1 John 5:4-5 – "for everyone who has been born of God overcomes the world..."

- Although death was defeated, we still face the day-to-day battles. We don't have the strength to fight against these powerful enemies on our own, so God gave us the power of the Holy Spirit.

2. **To strengthen us**
   - Remember the blessings we receive when we receive Christ as our Savior. (Chapter 3)
   - God's grace gives us the blessing of privilege and the blessing of power.
   - What is the difference in the two categories of grace? (Q #4)
   - What privilege? The privilege of being clothed with the Righteousness of Christ.
   - What power? Because of God's grace, we are blessed to have access to the Power of the Holy Spirit!
   - How are we empowered by the Holy Spirit? 2 Timothy 2:1 – "Be strengthened by the grace that is in Christ Jesus." (Paul is writing to Timothy here.)

     ...What does Paul mean by "be strengthened?"(Q #3) "Strengthened" is a "passive imperative" – indicates something done to us, not by us. So Timothy is to be strengthened by something outside himself.

     ...What is he strengthened by? "The grace that is in Christ Jesus." Christ's obedient life and death purchased every blessing God has for us!

     ...The grace we receive is because of what Christ did for us.

   - What does it mean to have access to the Power of the Holy Spirit?

     ...The blessings that God gives us through Christ are distributed and applied to us by the Holy Spirit.

     ...That is why Paul told the Ephesians in Ephesians 3:16, "Be strengthened with power through His Spirit in our inner being." We are strengthened by the power of the Holy Spirit!

   - What kind of power are we talking about? Romans 8:11 – "If the Spirit of Him who raised Jesus from the dead dwells in you, He who raised Christ Jesus from the dead will also give life to your mortal bodies through his Spirit who dwells in you." It is the same Power that raised Christ from the dead!

   - **How does this strength from the Holy Spirit play out in our lives?**

BREAK-OUT SESSION
2 Corinthians 12:9-10

> **TEACHER'S NOTE:**
> Break into groups to read 2 Corinthians 12:9-10 aloud at their tables and discuss Q #5 of the homework. Then reconvene and discuss the meaning of the passage one phrase at a time.

MEMORY VERSE

"My grace is sufficient for you, for my power is made perfect in weakness. Therefore, I will boast all the more gladly of my weakness, so that the power of Christ may rest upon me. (NASB "power of Christ may dwell in me.") For the sake of Christ, then, I am content with weaknesses, insults, hardships, persecutions, and calamities. For when I am weak, then I am strong." 2 Corinthians 12:9-10

- "My grace is sufficient for you." To what is Paul referring? The grace God gives you that blesses you with the power of the Holy Spirit is sufficient for you. It is all we need to face whatever comes our way!

- "For my power is made perfect in weakness." Christ's power can be most evident when we are at our weakest. When there can be no other explanation for your strength except only that which can be explained by the power of the Holy Spirit!

- "Therefore I will boast all the more gladly of my weaknesses." Why? "That the power of Christ may rest upon me." Paul is actually able to boast of his weakness so that the power of Christ can rest upon him! (NASB – So that the power of Christ can "dwell" in him!)

- "For the sake of Christ then, I am content with weakness, insults, hardships, persecutions and calamities…" Christ is glorified when people see in you a strength that comes only from Christ. Why can Paul be content? With what do you need be content?

- "For when I am weak, then I am strong." When we go through trials and weakness, Christ's power becomes apparent in our lives. When we are weak we can become strong because of the Power of the Holy Spirit!

- Just as we must look outside ourselves to the righteousness of Christ for our standing before God, we must also look outside ourselves to the power of the Holy Spirit for our strength to live the Christian life.

3. **To reveal himself to us**

    2 Corinthians 3:18 – "And we all with unveiled face, beholding the glory of the Lord, are being transformed into the same image from one degree of glory to another. For this comes from the Lord whose is the Spirit."

    - What does it mean to "behold the glory of God?" For a veil to be removed so you can see God's glory. (ESV Commentary)

    - It is only by the power of the Holy Spirit that our faces become "unveiled," that we are able to see God's glory, and are able to be transformed. Once again this happens as we get to know Him better through the reading of His Word.

4. **To sanctify us**

    Refer back to 2 Corinthians 3:18 – We "are being transformed into the same image from one degree of glory to another. For this comes from the Lord who is the Spirit."

- "Being transformed into the same image…" What is this process called? Sanctification. As our faces are unveiled and we see God's glory, we are being transformed and becoming more like Him. This is definitely a process and will not be complete until we see Him face to face.
- "For this comes from the Lord who is the Spirit." It is only by the power of the Holy Spirit that we can be transformed in our daily sanctification process.

5. **To Work in us** – The Holy Spirit applies His power in our lives in two ways

    Qualified Synergism – When He supplies us with all the enabling power, but we do all the tangible work

    - Philippians 2:13-14 – "It is God who works in you, both to will and to work for His good pleasure." (Q #11)

        …God provides us with both the motivation (the will) and the power (the work) to obey. The Power of the Holy Spirit relieves us from the burden of having insufficient will power and strength to obey God.

        TEACHER'S NOTE: Refer to pages 86-91 for further explanation of the Spirit's Monergistic and Synergistic work. (Q #10)

        …As He supplies the energy, with what does He equip us to do this work?

    - Hebrews 13:20-21 – "Now may the God of peace, who through the blood of the eternal covenant brought back from the dead our Lord Jesus, that great Shepherd of the sheep, equip you with everything good for doing His will, and may He work in us what is pleasing to Him, through Jesus Christ, to whom be glory for ever and ever. Amen."

        …What does He equip us with according to v. 21? "Everything good for doing His will." 1 Peter 4:10-11 states that "Each has received a gift, use it to serve one another." We serve by the strength that God supplies. (Q #11) These are **Spiritual gifts**.

        …What else does the Holy Spirit equip us with? **Fruit of the Spirit**… Galatians 5:22-23 –"love, joy, peace, patience, kindness, goodness, faithfulness, gentleness and self-control." It is only by the power of the Holy Spirit that we can have any of these qualities.

        …What does He equip us for? To do His will (Hebrews 13:21)

        …What is His will? To Proclaim His Word (Acts 1:8 – "You will receive power when the Holy Spirit has come upon you, and you will be my witnesses…to the ends of the earth.") and to Glorify Him (1 Peter 4:11 – "We serve with the strength God supplies…in order that in everything God may be glorified…")

    Monergistic Work – When the Holy Spirit helps us accomplish His agenda for our own spiritual growth without our effort and sometimes in spite of our effort – sometimes to accomplish things that are on His agenda.

    - What are some essentials of our Christian growth agenda that are only by the power of the Holy Spirit? (Q#12)

        …His work begins when He gives us new life by causing us to be born again. (John 3:5 talks about being "born of the Spirit.") We are justified when we first place our faith in what Christ did for us (justification). We are sealed with the Holy Spirit

...The process of recognizing our sin, going to the Gospel of grace, and then responding with gratitude

...Repentance and having Faith – Acts 11:18, Ephesians 2:8

...Obey – Ezekiel 36:27

...Motivation to be like Christ

...Assurance of our salvation – Romans 8:16 – "The Spirit himself bears witness...that we are Children of God."

> **TEACHER'S NOTE:**
> See page 89 for a great explanation of this process. The Heidelberg Catechism is structured around three "G"s: Our Guilt, God's Grace, Our response of Gratitude. (Q #13)

- Only by the power of the Holy Spirit can we live the Christian Life, repent, have faith, obey, have the motivation to be like Christ, and be assured that we are children of God (p. 88-89).

Sometimes it is difficult to understand where to draw the line between the Power of the Holy Spirit and our effort. The authors refer to this as **"The Seamless Application of Monergism and Synergism."** The best explanation of this is that "We are to work and apply ourselves with utmost seriousness and vigilance; but we're to do so with the recognition that God provides us the motivation and the power to obey" (p. 87-88).

What is our role?

Just like with the First Bookend with our renunciation and reliance, we need to renounce all confidence in our own power and then completely rely on the power of the Holy Spirit.

1. We don't merely need the help of the Holy Spirit to do this – we must be enabled.
2. We need to acknowledge that on our own we are helpless and then embrace reliance on the power of the Holy Spirit!

The Sovereignty of the Holy Spirit

1. God is in control and He manifests Himself through the power of the Holy Spirit according to His own timing! (Q #8)
2. Why do we sometimes feel like the Holy Spirit is not empowering us when we want Him to? (Q #9)
   - Maybe it is to remind us that without His enabling power, we can't fight sin, grow in character, or minister effectively. It drives us back to the cross and reminds us that no matter what are inadequacy is, we stand accepted before God because of the Righteousness of Christ – not because of our own ability.
   - Other times He dramatically manifests Himself through us when we are made fully aware of our own weakness and ability.

SUMMARY

We cannot live the life that God called us to without the Righteousness of Christ and the Power of the Holy Spirit. That is why this book is called "The Bookends of the *Christian Life*."

1. Both are "blood-bought, life-changing fountains of grace-blessings beyond measure" so that God gets all the glory. (p. 92)

2. What is the difference between them? (Q #14)

    - The Righteousness of Christ can never be changed. Because of what Christ did for us, nothing could ever make us more righteous or less righteous in our standing before God.

    - The Power of the Holy Spirit is always in process. It can never be finished and complete in our life until we see Him face to face. When we receive the Holy Spirit, we must respond to it and depend on it.

SONG

"In Me" by Casting Crowns

DISCUSSION TIME

Describe a time in your life when you have experienced the Power of the Holy Spirit and you know there is no other explanation for the work that was done in your life. Discuss questions 1, 6, and 7 from the homework.

LEADER'S GUIDE CHAPTER SEVEN

Dependent Responsibility

WELCOME and PRAYER

> **TEACHER'S NOTE:**
>
> Before you begin:
>
> 1. Write verses on the board for class to look up: Matthew 6:33; Ephesians 1:17-18; 1:19; 2 Timothy 3:16; Hebrews 4:12
> 2. Memory Verse: John 15:5
> 3. Song Lyrics

REVIEW

1. When we receive Christ as our personal Savior, we receive many blessings that come to us by His grace. We are not only blessed with the privileges that come with being clothed in the righteousness of Christ, but we have the blessing of being strengthened by the power of the Holy Spirit.

    - 2 Timothy 2:1 says, "Be strengthened by the grace that is in Christ Jesus." We are strengthened by something outside ourselves – the Power of the Holy Spirit.

    - The blessings that God gives us that are in Christ because of what He did for us are distributed and applied to us by the Holy Spirit.

2. God distributes His blessings to us through the Holy Spirit: to help us, strengthen us, reveal Himself to us, sanctify us, and work in us to accomplish His purpose.

3. How does the strength from the Holy Spirit play out in our lives?

    - MEMORY VERSE: 2 Corinthians 12:9-10 – "My grace is sufficient for you, for my power is made perfect in weakness. Therefore, I will boast all the more gladly of my weakness, so that the power of Christ may rest upon me. For the sake of Christ, then, I am content with weaknesses, insults, hardships, persecutions, and calamities. For when I am weak, then I am strong."

    - Sometimes it is through trials and weakness that Christ's power becomes most apparent in our lives. When we are weak, the power of the Holy Spirit can make us strong.

    - No matter what we are doing, whether it be struggling or serving God, none of it is possible without the power of the Holy Spirit.

4. Just as we must look outside ourselves to the righteousness of Christ to stand before God (First Bookend), we must also look outside ourselves to the power of the Holy Spirit for strength to live the Christian life.

5. When we receive the Holy Spirit, we must respond to Him and depend on Him.

LESSON 7: Dependent Responsibility

1. In responding to the work of the Holy Spirit, where do we draw the line between what we are responsible for, and being totally dependent on His power?

2. What does "dependent responsibility" mean? We are both dependent and responsible:

    - The dictionary definition of dependent is "to exist by virtue of a necessary relation."

    - We are responsible for being dependent on Him for everything!

BREAK-OUT SESSION

2 Timothy 2:15 and Colossians 1:29

> **TEACHER'S NOTE:**
> Have small groups read verses and discuss wha dependent responsibility looks like in scripture.

What does "dependent responsibility" look like in God's Word?

1. 2 Timothy 2:15 – "Do your best to present yourself to God as one approved, a worker who has no need to be ashamed."

    - What does it mean to "do your best?"

    - Page 96 – "Be diligent" or "Make every effort." Timothy's dependence on the Spirit did not take away his responsibility to work hard with the gifts God gave him.

    - We are to work diligently at our Christian growth with the assurance that God is at work in us.

2. Colossians 1:29 – "For this I toil, struggling with all His energy that He powerfully works within me." (Q #1)

    - What does toil mean? "Labor to the point of exhaustion"

    - What does struggling mean? A Greek word whose English definition is "to agonize."

    - Paul worked hard on his missionary journey to proclaim the Gospel and be all that God intended him to be.

    - With whose energy did Paul struggle? God's energy worked powerfully within Paul and works powerfully in us. Ephesians 1:19 – "And what is the immeasurable greatness of His power toward us who believe, according to the working of His great might."

3. The Holy Spirit's role is not to make our own energy unnecessary, but rather, effective.

Dependent Responsibility in our effort to grow in Christ-likeness

1. For what does God's Word say we are responsible?

    - Colossians 3:12-14 – God calls us to "Put on... compassionate hearts, kindness, humility, meekness, and patience, bearing with one another...forgiving each other..."

    - Galatians 5:16, 22-23 – Fruit of the Spirit – "Walk by the Spirit"

    - See p. 97 for other verses that refer to more responsibilities: "Watch and pray," "Be steadfast," "Train ourselves," "Make every effort" to grow in Christian character.

2. What do we notice about the verbs listed above?

    - They are moral imperatives, action statements, direct commands – not suggestions.

    - Commands from whom? 1 Thessalonians 4:3a – "For this is the will of God, your sanctification..." Paul is talking to the Thessalonians about the will of God – our sanctification – to make us more like Him!

3. All of the moral imperatives found in God's Word are not just good advice. They are direct commands from the creator of the universe – the very will of God.

4. Why do we sometimes gloss over these direct commands from God? We might not like what God is asking us to do because sometimes it is hard to follow His commands. How do we gloss over? Being selective of what we should and should not obey in scripture.

5. Look back at Galatians 5:16, 22-23 – "Walk by the Spirit…" The only way we can do what God is calling us to do is by the power of the Holy Spirit. It goes on to mention the Fruit of the Holy Spirit in verses 22-23 ("love, joy, peace, patience…."). It is often difficult and sometimes nearly impossible to have these qualities. We must remember they are only displayed in our lives through the Holy Spirit.

6. God has given us many commands in His Word. It is important to remember that this is why He gave us the enabling power of the Holy Spirit.

7. It is our responsibility to walk in obedience with the will of God and to work with 100% of our effort with the gifts He has given us. At the same time, we are to be 100% dependent on the Holy Spirit to enable us and make our work effective. The harder we work, the more we depend on the power of the Holy Spirit. (Q #2)

Means of Grace

1. What does this mean?
   - God uses different instruments to strengthen us by His grace.
   - We have the responsibility to respond to this grace through Spiritual Disciplines.
   - Through practicing the Spiritual Disciplines we gain access to His grace. (Q #3)

2. Two important truths (Q #4)
   - Spiritual disciplines are not the source of spiritual power, they are His instruments to transmit His power.
   - The practice of discipline doesn't earn us favor. (Christ did that for us when He died on the cross.) We can't fall into legalistic thinking – that somehow these disciplines will make us more righteous.

Spiritual Disciplines

We should not look at cultivating our relationship with God as a list of do's and don'ts. We have a responsibility to respond to the means of grace the Spirit provides to draw us closer to Him.

Daily Communion with God (Quiet Time)

1. Why do a Quiet Time?
   - It facilitates fellowship with God.
   - He calls us to spend time with Him. 1 Corinthians 1:9 – "God is faithful, by whom you were called into fellowship…"

2. What does fellowship with God look like in God's Word?
   - **MEMORY VERSE:** John 15:5 – "I am the vine; you are the branches. Whoever abides in me and I in him, he it is that bears much fruit, for apart from me you can do nothing." (ESV notes: "'Abide in me' means to continue in a daily, personal relationship with Jesus characterized by trust, prayer, obedience, and joy." We need to recognize that apart from Him, we can do nothing of external value.)

- Matthew 6:33 – "Seek first the kingdom of God and His righteousness, and all these things will be added to you." As we seek to know Him more, our knowledge of Him increases. As our knowledge of Him increases, the more we want to spend time with Him.
- Psalm 63 – "O God, you are my God; earnestly I seek you, my soul thirsts for you." When you love someone, you want to spend more time with him, Do we truly desire to be with Him?

3. Examples of Quiet Time: Bible reading, praying, journaling, listening to praise music, etc.

4. Important to note about spending time in God's Word:
   - Other ways we spend time with God cannot substitute for being in the Word.
   - There will be seasons where this is very difficult. When this happens, do whatever it takes to remind yourself of God's Word throughout the day, such as keeping the Bible open on the kitchen counter, posting Bible verses all over the house or in the car...
   - It is important to not just go through the motions. We need to take time to pray over and reflect on what we've read.
   - Pray what Paul prayed for the Ephesians: Ephesians 1:17,18 – "The God of our Lord Jesus Christ, the Father of glory, may give you a spirit of wisdom and of revelation in the knowledge of Him, having the eyes of your hearts enlightened, that you may know what is the hope to which He has called you."
   - Pray for wisdom and enlightenment. Ask Him to reveal what He wants you to learn. Take time to be quiet and listen to what He may have to say to you.

What are the essential aspects of daily communion with God?

1. **The Gospel**
   - Why the Gospel? It is the primary instrument of spiritual transformation!
   - 2 Corinthians 3:18 – "And we all, with unveiled face, beholding the glory of the Lord, are being transformed into the same image from one degree of glory to another. For this comes from the Lord who is the Spirit."
   - How do we behold the glory of God? (Q #6) The Holy Spirit helps us understand the Gospel by "lifting the veil." When we understand the Gospel, we see God's glory. As this happens, the Holy Spirit transforms us.
   - It is important for us to preach the Gospel to ourselves everyday. (Q #7) Begin each day by acknowledging that we are sinners and that God has made us alive with Christ, forgave us our sins, and cancelled our debt through the cross.
   - Find a passage that summarizes the Gospel and meditate on that. (Colossians 2:13-14)
   - As we understand the Gospel and remind ourselves of what Christ did for us daily, the Holy Spirit will motivate us to want to live our lives to glorify Him.

2. **All of Scripture**
   - Why the Bible?

...It is God's Word. All scripture is God breathed. 2 Timothy 3:16 says, "All scripture is breathed out by God and profitable for teaching, for reproof, for correction, and for training in righteousness."

...The Word of God is transforming. Hebrews 4:12 – "For the word of God is living and active, sharper than any two-edged sword, piercing to the division of soul and of spirit, of joints and of marrow, and discerning the thoughts and intentions of the heart." God's Word is alive, active, and convicting.

- What do we find in scripture? (Q #8)

    ...To know God's will. In Colossians 1:9-10, Paul prayed that the Colossian believers might "be filled with the knowledge of His will in all spiritual wisdom and understanding so as to walk in a manner worthy of the Lord, fully pleasing to him."

    ...Romans 12:2 – "Be transformed by the renewal of your mind, that by testing you may know what is the will of God." Scripture reveals His truth, and the Holy Spirit uses this truth to transform or sanctify us.

    ...To know the hope He has for us. Look back at Ephesians 1:17, Paul prayed this for the Ephesians that through "the knowledge of Him, having the eyes of your hearts enlightened, that you may know what is the hope to which He has called you…"

    ...To know the promises of His power and provision to help us carry out his will.

- Scripture is the only way to renew our minds. Do not rely on any book besides the Word of God for truth. It is ok to read other books as long as you don't replace the truth found in the Bible! Always compare what you are reading to God's Word. If it does not coincide, then it is not truth. Don't put your hope in it!
- God also reveals His Word to us through Bible-based preaching, Bible study, and scripture memorization.

3. **Prayer**

    - Why do we pray? To acknowledging our dependence on Him (Q #9) and our helplessness and inability to accomplish anything on our own.

    - When are we to pray? 1 Thessalonians 5:17 – "Pray without ceasing" (daily prayers and short, spontaneous prayers throughout the day)

    - What are we to pray for?

        ...To work in us and enable us to work. We can use a prayer journal or pray scripture. There are countless ways we can pray.

        ...Are we praying to get what we want or for God's will for our lives? It is not for us to question His will. We are to submit to and accept whatever He has for us.

        ...He always hears us and He always responds (yes, no, not yet)

        ...The more prayer, the more dependency – the more dependency, the more power.

4. **Circumstances**

    - We should continually reflect on the various circumstances that come our way.

    - Romans 8:28-29 – "And we know that in all things God works for the good of those who love Him, who have been called according to His purpose.

- God causes "all things" – circumstances, events, actions of other people (good or bad in our estimation) – to work together for our good and His glory. (Q #10)

    ...Our good? Conformity to the image of His Son (sanctification).

    ...His glory? He uses all circumstances, good and bad, to accomplish His will, which will ultimately give Him glory.

- As we reflect on our challenging circumstances, we should ask God how He wants to use them in our lives. We should also make a habit of recognizing that good circumstances are only by God's grace and mercy.

SUMMARY

1. We need to depend on the power of the Holy Spirit, but we have a responsibility as well.
2. Communion with God needs to be a daily practice and our heart's desire. This will only happen with the power of the Holy Spirit. (Q #11-12)

SONG

"I Will Abide" by Christ for the Nations and Lauren Farmer

DISCUSSION TIME

What can you do to improve the quality of your daily communion with the Lord?

LEADER'S GUIDE CHAPTER EIGHT

The Help of the Divine Encourager

WELCOME and PRAYER

REVIEW

1. We learned what "**Dependent Responsibility**" means in our walk with Christ.
   - It is our responsibility to walk in obedience with the will of God and to work with 100% of our effort with the gifts He has given us.
   - At the same time, we are to be 100% dependent on the Holy Spirit to enable us and make our work effective.

2. We learned about "**Means of Grace**"
   - God uses different instruments to strengthen us by His grace.
   - We have the responsibility to respond to this grace that He provides by participating in different spiritual disciplines such as prayer, spending time in God's word etc. As we participate in these spiritual disciplines we are responding to His call to depend on Him by abiding in Him.

3. Memory Verse: John 15:5 – "I am the vine; you are the branches. Whoever abides in me and I in him, he it is that bears much fruit, for apart from me you can do nothing." We need to recognize the importance of daily communion with God and abiding in Him. Apart from Him, we can do nothing!

The Help of the Divine Encourager

1. Why do we need the help of the Divine Encourager? Because we still face a daily battle with sin.

2. Why do we still have to battle sin?

3. "Already not yet phenomenon"

   - Although we are free from condemnation, we still battle with sin until the day we see Jesus face to face. We are already perfect in our standing before Christ and in our position as being justified, but not yet in our day-to-day experience.

   - Although we are free from condemnation…

     …Romans 8:1 – "There is, therefore, now no condemnation for those who are in Christ Jesus."

     …Romans 6:14 – "For sin will have no dominion over you, since you are not under the law but under grace."

   - But we will still battle with sin…

     …Galatians 5:17 – "For the desires of the flesh are against the Spirit, and the desires of the Spirit are against the flesh, for these are opposed to each other, to keep you from doing the things you want to do."

> **TEACHER'S NOTE:**
> There is often a question amongst believers regarding the fact that if we already stand righteous before God, why do we still battle with sin? Discussing the "Already not yet Phenomenon" helps us understand why we still face a daily battle with sin and why we need the help of the Divine Encourager.

...What are "desires of the flesh?" Our sinful nature...the desire to do anything outside of God's will. Our flesh is enmity (a state of being actively opposed to someone) against God as long as we are in this flesh.

...When we receive our new body, we will be free from sin.

- Why are the "desires of the Spirit...against the flesh and they are opposed to each other?"

    ..."To keep us from doing the things we want to do." The desires of our flesh pull us away from the desires of the Spirit in a constant battle.

    ...Romans 7:15 – "For I do not understand my own actions. For I do not do what I want, but I do the very thing I hate." Sometimes we think we've got a certain sin knocked only to find ourselves slipping back into temptation.

4. It is clear that we need the Power of the Holy Spirit to help us fight this ever-present battle with sin!

How does the Holy Spirit help us battle sin?

1. The Holy Spirit gives us HOPE.

    MEMORY VERSE – Romans 15:13 – "May the God of hope fill you with all joy and peace in believing, so that by the power of the Holy Spirit you may abound in hope."

2. What kind of Hope?

    - The Hope that God gave us a Helper (John 14:16) to walk with us and empower us through this battle. Galatians 5:16 says, "But I say, walk by the Spirit, and you will not gratify the desires of the flesh." The Holy Spirit reminds us to depend on His strength as we go through the sanctification process in our daily battle with sin.

    - The Hope that God is at work in us. Philippians 2:13 – "...it is God who works in you, both to will and to work for His good pleasure." He's not finished with us yet!

    - The Holy Spirit gives us the Hope of Righteousness (Q#2). Galatians 5:5 says, "For through the Spirit, by faith, we ourselves eagerly wait for the hope of righteousness." The Holy Spirit points us to the Righteousness of Christ, reminding us that we do not have to produce perfect righteousness by our own efforts. Because of what Christ did for us, we can stand righteous before our God.

3. Why does Galatians 5:5 say that we "eagerly wait for the hope of righteousness?"

    - We "wait eagerly" for God to complete His righteousness in us when we see Him face to face when we die or when Christ returns.

    - This is where the "Not Yet" part of the phenomenon fits in. Ephesians 1:13-14 – We "were sealed with the promised Holy Spirit, who is the guarantee of our inheritance until we acquire possession of it..." God gave us the Holy Spirit to help us in the battle until we see Him face to face - until the redemption of those who are God's possession.

        ...Not the redemption in its first stage. Galatians 3:13 – "We were redeemed from the curse of the law." We are already redeemed by the blood of Christ. Our title is secured. We have been paid for. We are sons and daughters. We are already perfect in our standing before our God.

Romans 8:23 – "But we ourselves, who have the first fruits of the Spirit, groan inwardly as we wait eagerly for adoption as sons, the redemption of our bodies." We "eagerly await" for the fulfillment of our adoption - when our bodies are redeemed and raised from the dead!

4. The Holy Spirit gives us hope in our battle with sin as we wait eagerly for the day when we are with Him and delivered from the battle once and for all. As we wait, the Holy Spirit encourages us.

Four ways the Holy Spirit encourages us:

The spirit encourages us to renew our dependence on the second bookend by remembering the first: Life-changing Gratitude for Purchased Grace.

BREAKOUT SESSION

1. **Life-changing Gratitude for Purchased Grace**

The Holy Spirit enables us to have life-changing gratitude

What happens as a result of the Holy Spirit living inside us and encouraging us?

> **TEACHER'S NOTE:** Have groups read verses in italics and then answer question below. Then reconvene for class discussion.

- John 15:26 – "When the Helper comes, He will bear witness about me." (Q#3) The Holy Spirit opens our hearts to the Gospel. 2 Corinthians 3:18 – "Beholding the Glory of the Lord." The Holy Spirit lifts the veil so we are able to see the Gospel!

- John 14:26 – "...he will bring to your remembrance all that I have said to you." He reminds us of His truth that we have heard, read, or memorized and stirs within us a huge sense of gratitude that transforms us at the very core of our being. (Q #4)

- 2 Corinthians 5:14-15 – "For the love of Christ controls us, because we have concluded this: that one has died for all, therefore all have died;" (Q #5)

  ...What about the Gospel motivates us? The love for Christ or the love of Christ? The love OF Christ!

  ...What kind of love controls us? "Because one has died for all, therefore, all have died." It's the kind of love that caused Him to give up His own life for us! When Christ died to pay for our sins, it was as if we all died.

  ...Why did He die? (See the rest of 2 Corinthians 5:14-15) V. 15 "that those who live might no longer live for themselves but for Him who for their sake died and was raised." That we would no longer live for ourselves, but for Him!! It's not about us! How many times do we need to remind ourselves of this!

- 1 John 4:9-10, 19 – "In this the love of God was made manifest among us, that God sent His only Son, into the world, so that we might live through Him. In this is love, not that we have loved God but that He loved us and sent His Son to be the propitiation for our sins...We love because He first loved us." (Q#5)

  ...Why did God send His only Son in to the world? So that we might live through Him! To be the propitiation for our sins

  ...What does propitiation mean? Propitiation means "wrath bearer." He bore the wrath of God for us!

Our gratitude for the love that provided the first bookend (the Righteousness of Christ) encourages us to depend on the second bookend (the Power of the Holy Spirit) for the strength to obey His commandments and live the Christian life.

As our understanding of Christ's love increases, our gratitude increases! That is why we need to be in God's Word and "preach the Gospel to ourselves" daily. The Holy Spirit will renew our motivation to live for Christ.

2. **The Explusion Power of a New Affection**

    - How do we battle against the sins of our heart?

      ...The Old Paradigm – what I should do fights my sinful desire of what I want to do – very limited success.

      ...The New Paradigm – We must replace the object of our sinful affection with God himself. Based on Thomas Chalmers' sermon on the expulsive power of a new affection. (Q#6) The intensity of our new affection for Christ weakens and sometimes destroys the power of sin in our hearts.

    - We must battle desire with desire. Whichever desire is the strongest will determine the outcome of the battle. (Q #7) Galatians 5:17 – "For the desire of the flesh are against the Spirit, and the desires of the Spirit are against the flesh, for these are opposed to each other, to keep you from doing the things you want to do." Our Godly desires must overcome our sinful desires if we're to obey God.

    - How do we win the battle against sin? We must strengthen and encourage our godly desires. How do we strengthen our godly desires? By simultaneously growing in our awareness of:

      ...Our sin: our knowledge of the moral will of God and how far short we fall daily.

        - How does the Holy Spirit do this? John 16:8 states that when the Helper comes "He will convict the world concerning sin and righteousness."

        - As our awareness of our sin increases, the immensity of the gap between what we deserve and what Christ purchased for us widens. (Q #8)

      ...God's love – We need to remind ourselves of the amazing grace and blessings purchased by Christ's death on the cross.

        - His love for us is so great that "while we were still sinners, Christ died for us!" – Romans 5:8

        - We need to truly "grasp how wide and long and high and deep is the love of Christ" – Ephesians 3:18-19

        - As our desperate need for the Gospel and awareness of His amazing love *increases*, our *sinful desires weaken* and are *replaced* with a new desire for God. "Because Christ loves me so much, I love him more than_____." (p.115)

        - Our love for God is then expressed in personal obedience and a deepened relationship with Him.

3. **Enjoying the Relationship**

    - Westminster Confession of Faith – What is the purpose of life? "The chief end of man is to glorify God and enjoy Him forever." What does it mean to enjoy Him? (Q #9) To experience an active and intimate relationship with Him.

    - Because of the Gospel we can have a relationship with the Creator of the universe! Matthew 27:51 – When Christ died, "the curtain of the temple was torn in two, from top to bottom." Hebrews 4:16 – "So we can "approach the throne of grace with confidence." 1 Peter 3:18 – "Christ suffered once for sins, the righteous for the unrighteous, that He might bring us to God."

    - Because of our union with Christ, the Father loves us as He loves the Son. John 17:22-23 is the prayer Jesus prayed before He entered the garden of Gethsemane on the night before His death: "The glory that you have given me I have given to them, that they may be one even as we are one, I in them and you in me, that they may become perfectly one, so that the world may He loves us as He loved His own Son!

    > **TEACHER'S NOTE:**
    > Great illustration - Sara Groves (Christian singer/song writer) sang in her song *Hello Lord*, "I know that you tore the veil so I could sit with you in person and hear what you're saying."

    - How does enjoying a relationship with God help battle against sin? (Q #11) The Holy Spirit uses our appetite for enjoying our relationship with God to battle against our sinful desires. Is it worth turning our backs on God to enjoy sin's fleeting pleasures? In Hebrews 11:25, Moses would rather be ill-treated with the people of God than to enjoy the fleeting pleasures of sin. A relationship with God is so enjoyable that it makes other pleasures appear small in comparison.

4. **The Promises of God**

    How does the Holy Spirit point us to His Truth and the Promises of God?

    - The Holy Spirit points us to truth. John 16:13 – "When the Spirit of Truth comes, He will guide you into all truth." What is truth?

        …John 14:6 – "I am the way, the truth." The Spirit points us to Jesus who is the source of our righteousness for justification. Jesus is truth.

        …John 17:17 – "Your word is truth." The Spirit points us to the truth in God's Word to help us battle sin and to guide us in becoming more like Christ. God's Word it truth.

    - The Holy Spirit leads us to specific promises of God.

        …The promises equip us for our moment-to-moment battles with sin or what we will face in the future. (Q #12) 2 Peter 1:4 – "He has granted to us His precious and very great promises, so that through them you may become partakers of the divine nature, having escaped from the corruption that is in the world because of sinful desire." Become partakers? His Word gives us the assurance that He'll fulfill His promises in His own perfect timing.

        …His promises point us toward the hope of heaven and eternal life. John 16:13 – "The Spirit of Truth…will declare to you the things that are to come." 1 Corinthians 2:9-10 – "What no eye has seen, nor ear has heard….what God has prepared for those who love Him."

        …His promises empower us to walk through the most difficult trials and glorify God in the process. Deuteronomy 31:8 – "The Lord Himself goes before you and will be with you, He will never leave you nor forsake you, do not be afraid, do not be discouraged."

What is our role?

1. We have the responsibility to respond to God's grace by participating in different spiritual disciplines (Chapter 7), such as:

    - Spending time in the Word daily
    - Scripture Memorization
    - Journaling

2. Store His promises in our heart so we can be equipped for whatever comes our way.

SONG

"Strong Enough" by Matthew West

DISCUSSION TIME

1. To what spiritual disciplines can you commit to prepare yourself for your future needs? (Q #13)

2. What are some of the promises from God's Word that the Spirit has used to motivate or encourage you in your walk? (Q #14)

LEADER'S GUIDE CHAPTER NINE

GOSPEL ENEMY #3: Self-Reliance

WELCOME and PRAYER

REVIEW

1. **Why do we need the help of the Divine Encourager?** Although we are free from condemnation, we still face a daily battle with sin.

2. **"Already not yet" Phenomenon** – We are perfect in our standing before Christ as being justified, but we still battle sin on this earth. That is why God gave us the Holy Spirit.

3. **The Holy Spirit gives us hope for the battle**, which leads us to our MEMORY VERSE: Romans 15:13 – "May the God of hope fill you with all joy and peace in believing, so that by the power of the Holy Spirit you may abound in hope."

4. **Four ways the Holy Spirit encourages us**:
   - Life-changing gratitude for purchased grace
   - The expulsive power of a new affection – our Godly desires must overcome our sinful if we're to obey God. This is only possible by the power of the Holy Spirit.
   - Enjoying the relationship – The Holy Spirit uses our growing appetite for enjoying our relationship with God to battle against our sinful desires.
   - The promises of God – The Holy Spirit points us to His Truth and the Promises found in His word.

Gospel Enemy #3: Self-Reliance

1. What are some examples of self-reliance in today's society? "Just do it." "Pull yourself up by your bootstraps." "You can do it!"

2. What does the world say about self-reliance? (Q #2)
   - We need to be self-confident and self-sufficient to be successful.
   - Good self-esteem is one of the greatest virtues.
   - We must learn to be independent – relying on no one but ourselves.

3. Why do you think the world is so self-reliant? (Q #1)
   - This concept has been force fed to us since we were born. How? Parents, teachers, coaches, motivational seminars, TV, movies, advertising, self-help books such as "The Power of Positive Thinking," etc.
   - It's been embedded in our minds – if we just try hard enough we can accomplish anything.

What is wrong with being self-reliant?

It is Not Biblical

1. When we are self-reliant we are sinning. God wants us to rely on Him and when we don't we are essentially disobeying Him and depending on something else We are redirecting our dependency onto an object of faith outside of the power of the Holy Spirit. We need to humbly remember what our position is in our relationship with God.

   - John 15:5 – "Apart from me you can do nothing." (Q #3) We as Christians are dependent on the power of the Holy Spirit to live the Christian life and bear spiritual fruit. We can do nothing of eternal value without Him.
   - Acts 17:28 – "In Him we live, move and exist." Every thing we do, every part of our life, our ability to think, breathe, etc...it all comes from God.
   - Corinthians 4:7 – "What do you have that you did not receive? If then you received it, why do you boast as if you did not receive it?" (Q #4) Every thing we have has been given to us. All of our abilities, opportunities, and blessings are from God.

2. God's Word says that our human strength is insufficient to live the Christian life. We cannot be who God has called us to be without the Power of the Holy Spirit. When we try to live the Christian life on our own strength it can lead to sin.

It is a Gospel Enemy

1. When we rely only on ourselves, we are being self-reliant towards God because we are depending on our own power, not the power of the Holy Spirit.

2. The authors compare self-reliance with self-righteousness in the first Bookend (Q #2): Self-righteousness is the opposite of dependence on Christ's righteousness for justification. We think we earn our salvation by good works. Self-reliance is the opposite of dependence on the Holy Spirit's power for sanctification. We assume we grow spiritually by our own effort and willpower.

3. When we are not relying on the power of the Holy Spirit, we are nullifying the Gospel. When we are self-reliant, we're denying the very power that raised Christ from the grave. Romans 8:11 – "If the Spirit of Him who raised Jesus from the dead dwells in you, He who raised Christ Jesus from the dead dwells in you." It is only by the grace of God and Christ's death on the cross that we even have access to the power of the Holy Spirit!

4. Therefore, we need to rely on the power of the Holy Spirit for everything God calls us to be – in our job, family, daily routine, even our spiritual disciplines.

Self-Reliance in the Bible

1. Paul talks about the Romans exchanging God's truth for a lie and relying on their own truth.

   - Romans 1:25, 28 NASB – "For they exchanged the truth of God for a lie, and worshiped and served the creature rather than the Creator, who is blessed forever...God gave them over to a depraved mind."
   - What happened when the Romans started relying on their own truth and what they wanted to believe? God gave them over to a depraved mind. Definition of depraved: "morally corrupt."
   - When we don't acknowledge God any longer, we can end up "morally corrupt!"

2. Peter

    - Matthew 26:31-35 – Before Jesus' crucifixion He said, "You will all fall away because of me this night…" Peter responded, "Though they all fall away because of you, I will never fall away." Jesus countered that before the rooster crowed, Peter would deny Him three times. Peter retorted, "Even if I must die with you, I will not deny you!"

    - What was Peter's object of dependence? What was he depending on? (Q #6) His own will power. "I will never fall away; I will not deny you." He thought he would have the strength to stand where others would fall.

    - Luke 22:60-63 – Peter denied Jesus three times before the rooster crowd. Then Peter remembered what Jesus had said, he felt convicted and "wept bitterly." He realized he did not have the strength on his own to stand strong for Jesus.

Self-Reliance in our Lives

1. How often do we rely on our own strength in order to remain faithful to Jesus?

    - When this happens what is our object of dependence? Ourselves!

    - Where do people who don't know Christ think their strength comes from? What kinds of things do they do? Example: Those that use Yoga to find the strength and power within themselves.

2. What does it look like when we try to live the Christian life by our own strength?

    - Self-imposed demands or guidelines about how to be a good Christian. "But I go to church every Sunday." "But I pray every day."

    - What happens when we do this? It can lead to pride, frustration, legalism, even a ship-wreck of faith. 1 Corinthians 10:12 – "Let anyone who thinks he stands take heed lest he falls."

    - When we perceive we've succeeded on our own, and met our own criteria, we take credit and steal God's glory in the process. We think, "I do the work, I get the credit, not God." We must remember we are a created being from a higher power and are to give Him all the glory!

    - Ironically, the more God-given natural abilities we have, the more prone we are to rely on them rather than God. We take them for granted. We forget that our gifts and success are only by the grace of God. Once again, we take all the credit.

    - When we rely on our own strength, in the slightest way, in order to remain faithful to Jesus, we deny that our strength is imperfect and the Holy Spirit's strength is flawless.

3. Where does God's Word say our strength comes from?

    - Psalm 121:1-2 – "I lift up my eyes to the hills. From where does my help come? My help comes from the LORD, who made heaven and earth."

    - In the Message Translation – "My strength comes from the Lord."

BREAKOUT SESSION

Biblical Dependence – Paul

One of the most frequently quoted motivational Bible verses is Philippians 4:13 – "I can do all things through Christ who strengthens me." But this verse can be taken out of context. We need to look further into Paul's circumstances to better understand what he is referring to.

> **TEACHER'S NOTE:**
> Have groups read 2 Corinthians 11:25, 27, then read Philippians 4:11-13. Discuss how Paul shifted his dependence back onto the power of the Holy Spirit despite his circumstances. Then reconvene and discuss as a class.

1. Paul had undergone severe persecution and trials during his missionary journeys. He was writing this from prison. Let's look at some of his hardships.

    - 2 Corinthians 11:25, 27 – "Three times I was beaten with rods. Once I was stoned. Three times I was shipwrecked; a night and a day I was adrift at sea…in toil and hardship, through many a sleepless night, in hunger and thirst, often without food, in cold and exposure."

2. Now lets look at the verses that come before Philippians 4:13.

    - Philippians 4:11-12 – "For I have learned to be content whatever the circumstances. I know what it is to be in need, and I know what it is to have plenty. I have learned the secret of being content in any and every situation, whether well fed or hungry, whether living in plenty or in want."

    - What issue was Paul dealing with? "To be content" (v. 11). Content in what? "Whatever the circumstances!" Remember, Paul had to "learn" to be content." It is a process! It is often only in hardship that God can even teach us contentment.

3. Look again at verse 13 – "I can do all things through Him who gives me strength." (Q #7) What does Paul mean by "all things"? Through strength from Christ, Paul learned to be content with all the circumstances God allowed in his life. What does this mean for us? Obedience to God…all that is in His will. How can we do this? By the power of the Holy Spirit! Remember from Chapter 6 – if God has called you, He "will equip you with everything good for doing his will…" Hebrews 13:20-21.

4. **MEMORY VERSE**: 2 Corinthians 3:4-6 – "Such is the confidence that we have through Christ toward God. Not that we are sufficient in ourselves to claim anything as coming from us, but our sufficiency is from God…who has made us ministers of the new covenant…" (Q #7)

5. Our sufficiency to be an effective minister of the Gospel comes from Him and Him alone!

How does the Holy Spirit help free us from self-reliance?

1. By revealing our sinfulness: From John Newton's letters (Q #9)

    - When we acknowledge that our hearts are deceitful and our lives are full of weakness, stubbornness, ingratitude, foolishness, the Holy Spirit reminds us that none of this can separate us from the love of God. How do we know this? Romans 8:38-39 – "For I am sure that neither death nor life, nor angels nor rulers, nor things present nor things to come, nor powers, nor height nor depth, nor anything else in all creation, will be able to separate us from the love of God in Christ Jesus our Lord."

    - We recognize that when we've wandered or have fallen, He has been there to pick us up – from the moment we received Him as Savior and He redeemed us, to every time we fall. Psalm 40:1-2 – "I waited patiently for the LORD; He turned to me and heard my cry. He lifted me out of the slimy pit, out of the mud and mire; He set my feet on a rock and gave me a firm place to stand."

65

- The pain brought about by recognizing our sinfulness weakens our self-reliance. The Holy Spirit points us to the cross reminding us that it is Christ's death that paid for our sin. He died the death we should have died. Galatians 2:20 – "I have been crucified with Christ. It is no longer I who live, but Christ who lives in me." He points us to His power that reminds us we have a Helper that will give us strength to turn from sin and live more like Him.
- So as the Holy Spirit reminds us of our sin and our insufficient strength to live the Christian life on our own, we are reminded of our desperate need for Him.

2. By helping us accept the "thorn" in our flesh

- Sometimes God allows certain challenging circumstances in our lives to remind us that in our weakness, we can rely on the all-sufficiency of the Power of the Holy Spirit.
- Let's go back to Paul. We know that along his missionary journey he endured much persecution, hardship, and many sleepless nights. But God also blessed him with amazing visions and revelations (2 Corinthians 12:2-3).
- 2 Corinthians 12:7-8 – (Q #10) "So to keep me from becoming conceited because of the surpassing greatness of the revelations, a thorn was given me in the flesh, a messenger of Satan to harass me, to keep me from becoming conceited. Three times I pleaded with the Lord about this, that it should leave me."
- Why was he given this thorn in his flesh? To keep him from becoming conceited because of the greatness of the revelations he received.
- What do you think the thorn was? We don't know what his thorn was or whether it was physical or emotional. It must have been painful because Paul begged three times for the Lord to take it away. Did God remove the thorn? No!
- 2 Corinthians 12:9a – (Q #11) "God said to me, 'My grace is sufficient for you, for my power is made perfect in weakness." God promised that His Grace would be sufficient for Paul and His power would be made perfect in Paul's weakness. So instead of relying on his own flesh, Paul embraced the power of Christ revealed to him through his weakness. (Q #13) Paul's weakness, not his revelations, were used as the platform to demonstrate the power of the Holy Spirit.
- 2 Corinthians 12:9b – "I will boast all the more gladly of my weaknesses….For when I am weak, then I am strong." God-reliance took the place of self-reliance with Paul. In his weakness, he realized that his own strength was insufficient. This enabled Paul to completely rely on the power of the Holy Spirit to serve God. Philippians 3:14 – "I press on toward the goal for the prize of the upward call of God in Christ Jesus."

Whether it is in our sin or in challenging circumstances, we need to remember that our strength is imperfect and embrace the Power of the Holy Spirit whose strength is flawless.

SONG

"Holy Spirit Have Your Way" by Leeland

DISCUSSION TIME

1. Read Matthew 26:31-35. What was the object of Peter's dependence? In what ways do our acts of self-reliance resemble Peter's denial of Christ? (Q #6)

2. When we fall into a pattern of self-reliance, how can the truth from Philippians 4:13 and 2 Corinthians 3:5-6 shift our dependence back on the power of the Holy Spirit? (Q #7)

3. What are you dealing with right now where you need to embrace the power of the Holy Spirit – like Paul did?

LEADER'S GUIDE CHAPTER TEN

Leaning on the Second Bookend

WELCOME and PRAYER

REVIEW

1. **Why is self-reliance wrong?**

    - It is not biblical. Apart from Him we can do nothing. We were meant to have an intimate relationship with God, and being self-reliant draws us further away from Him and can ultimately lead to sin.

    - It is a Gospel enemy. When we are not relying on the power of the Holy Spirit, we are essentially nullifying the Gospel. We're denying the very power that raised Christ from the grave! Self-reliance causes us to take all the credit when we succeed and steal God's glory in the process.

2. From where does God's Word say our strength comes?

    - Psalm 121:1-2 says our "strength comes from the Lord!"

    - MEMORY VERSE: 2 Corinthians 3:4-6 – "Such is the confidence that we have through Christ toward God. Not that we are sufficient in ourselves to claim anything as coming from us, but our sufficiency is from God, who has made us ministers of the new covenant…"

    - Our sufficiency to be who God calls us to be comes from Him and Him alone.

3. Instead of relying on our own flesh, we need to embrace the power of the Holy Spirit that can be revealed to us through our weakness - like Paul did in 2 Corinthians 12:9 – "For when I am weak, then I am strong."

Chapter Ten: Leaning on the Second Bookend

Even though we are well aware of the Power of the Holy Spirit, what do we have a tendency of doing?

1. Lean on our own strength instead! We lean our books on our own "bookends:" our natural abilities, our strength, and our resources.

2. How do we fight this natural tendency?

    - We need to constantly remind ourselves of the greatness of the Power of the Holy Spirit by "seeing" with the eyes of our hearts. (chapter 5)

    - Ephesians 1:18-19 – "Having the eyes of your heart enlightened that you may know…what immeasurable greatness of His power toward us who believe, according to the working of His great might." A greater understanding of His power shifts our dependence away from our own strength and onto the Holy Spirit.

Three Focal Points for Shifting our Dependence to the Second Bookend

Focal Point #1: Our Desperate Weakness

1. The authors use Isaiah 41:14-16 to portray how God transforms our desperate weakness into a powerful tool for Him.

2. Isaiah 41:14 – "Fear not, you worm Jacob, you men of Israel! I am the one who helps you, declares the Lord; your Redeemer is the Holy One of Israel."

    - Who do you think God is speaking to? God is speaking to His discouraged chosen people in the Old Testament. He is consoling Jacob and the Jewish exiles in Babylon (6th century).

    - Why do you think God calls Jacob a worm? (Q #2) Apart from receiving God's enabling power, we're as helpless as worms!

3. Isaiah 41:15-16 – "Behold, I make of you a threshing sledge, new, sharp, and having teeth; you shall thresh the mountains and crush them and you shall make the hills like chaff...And you shall rejoice in the Lord; in the Holy One of Israel you shall glory."

    - What can happen when we shift our dependence to the second bookend? God makes of us a "threshing sledge." A threshing sledge is a powerful tool used to harvest crops (ESV Study Bible definition).

    - The Holy Spirit transforms "the worm" into a useful, powerful too. – a threshing sledge that crushes mountains. When He transforms us from useless worms into powerful tools for Him, we get the joy, and God gets the glory!

4. Seeing ourselves as weak and helpless is a necessary step in shifting our dependence from our strength to His. We need to stop relying on our own power before we're able to receive power from the Holy Spirit.

Focal Point #2: The Reliable Power of the Holy Spirit

1. We need to focus on the reliable power of the Holy Spirit in our sanctification process and in the daily spiritual battles we face.

2. Progressive sanctification (Q #3) – What do we know about sanctification?

    - It is the continual process of becoming more like Him. It starts at the point in time when we are justified by trusting Christ as our Savior and ends at the moment we depart from our physical body and see Him face to face.

    - Progressive sanctification encompasses everything in our lives, both spiritual and temporal. 1 Thessalonians 5:23 – "Now may the God of peace Himself sanctify you completely, and may your whole spirit and soul and body be kept blameless at the coming of our Lord Jesus Christ."

    - We need to truly trust that the Holy Spirit has the power to change our life no matter what we are going through. Do you really believe the Holy Spirit can change your life?

3. What does the process of sanctification involve? (Q #4)

    - The process of this transformation into Christ-likeness involves "seeing Him" with the eyes of our heart. 2 Corinthians 3:18 from Ch 6 – "And we all, with unveiled face, beholding the glory of the Lord, are being transformed into the same image from one degree of glory to another..."

- How do we "see Him"? By daily being in God's Word and spending time with Him. When we spend a lot time with someone, we begin to pick up traits from that person. As we spend more time with God, we will see the glory of the Lord more, and we will become more like Him.

4. So when we combine 1 Thessalonians 5:23 and 2 Corinthians 3:18, we see that our sanctification is a God-centered process mediated by the power of the Holy Spirit. We need to remember to rely on His power to help us become more like Him!

5. What is happening when we depend fully on God and He seems unresponsive? (Q #5)

    - As we depend on the Power of the Holy Spirit, He transforms us according to His plan and timetable. Rarely, if ever, according to our timetable.
    - In His infinite wisdom and mercy, He empowers only what is best for us – for our good and His glory (Romans 8:28).

6. Depending fully on the Holy Spirit does not mean that we will always get what we want.

    - Hebrews 11 speaks of many "Heroes of Faith" mentioned throughout the Bible. Although their faith was strong, their outcomes weren't always wonderful. "Some were tortured…stoned…sawn in two" (vs. 35-37). "Though commended through their faith, did not receive what was promised, since God had provided something better for us, that apart from us they should not be made perfect" (vs. 39-40).

> **GOING A LITTLE DEEPER…**
> The "Heroes of Faith" did not receive what was promised because Jesus had not come yet. But they still had faith that God's promise would be fulfilled. Remember Hebrews 11 starts out with "Now faith is the assurance of things hoped for, the conviction of things not seen." How much greater should our faith be that we are among the New Testament Saints – knowing that there are actual witnesses to Jesus' death and resurrection! This is a reminder to us that apart from the Gospel we cannot become perfect. Because Jesus is the completion of God's promise!

    - We can rest assured that we can rely on the Holy Spirit to accomplish all of His divine intentions and in the meantime we can be transformed into a mighty tool for Him!

BREAKOUT SESSION

7. Remember, as long as we are on this earth, we will face daily spiritual battles, but we don't have to fight it with our own power! (Q #6)

> **TEACHER'S NOTE:**
> How does the truth from 2 Corinthians 10:3-4 and Philippians 1:6 give you hope for these battles?

    - 2 Corinthians 10:3-4 – "For though we walk in the flesh, we are not waging war according to the flesh. For the weapons of our warfare are not of the flesh, but have divine power to destroy strongholds." *(Definition of "stronghold": A faulty thinking pattern based on lies and deception.)*
    - What are the weapons of our warfare that have divine power? "Take up the whole armor of God…to stand firm." Ephesians 6:13-20 – The Shield of Faith, The Sword of the Spirit (Word of God), Helmet of Salvation, Breastplate of righteousness etc…
    - God provides us with armor that will cover us from head to toe so that we have complete protection from the enemy and are ready for battle! Through the weapons empowered by the Holy Spirit, He can destroy our strongholds of sin – whether it is wrong thinking, behavior, or whatever your stronghold might be!

- Remember Jesus never said it would be easy. John 16:33 – "In this world, you will have trouble…" But He promises us…"Fear not…I have overcome the world!"
- Philippians 1:6 – "I am sure of this, that He who began a good work in you will bring it to completion at the day of Jesus Christ." (Q #6) He promises He will complete this sanctification process in us!

Focal Point #3: Rejection of Self-Reliance

1. It is fairly easy to detect our own self-reliance. (See questions p. 140 as a good reminder.) The challenge is rejecting it. "To kill poison ivy, or self-reliance, you have to get it by the roots" (p.141).

2. What is at the root of self-reliance? (Q #7) Pride!
    - Genesis 3:5-6 – In the garden, the serpent tempted Adam and Eve by saying, "You will be like God." What became their motivation? To "be like God."
    - Isaiah 14:12-14 (KJV) – Lucifer declares, "I will make myself like the Most High." He wanted to be glorified and he didn't want to submit to God. Instead, he wanted to be like God.
    - When we are being self-reliant, we are essentially wanting to be our own god. We don't think we need God and that's why we end up relying on ourselves. When we succeed, we want the credit, attention, and the glory. This is a pride issue! We are making a "declaration of independence" apart from God, and this is the root of sin nature in all of us.

    > **TEACHER'S NOTE:**
    > Read Isaiah 14:12-14 in its entirety for context: "How art thou fallen from heaven, O Lucifer, …I will ascend into Heaven, I will exalt my throne above the stars of God. I will ascend above the heights of the clouds; I will be like the most High."

3. Self-reliance is at the root of all three Gospel enemies!
    - **Self-reliance** – I can do it myself.
    - **Self-righteousness** – I am my own god. I determine what's right and wrong. I declare myself as "good enough."
    - **Persistent Guilt** – I refuse to acknowledge and embrace the solution God has provided for my sin dilemma. I will be my own judge.

4. How do we reject self-reliance?
    - Making a daily declaration that "God is God, and I am not" and "killing" self-reliance at the root.

        …Colossians 3:9 – "…Put off the old self with its practices and… put on the new self, which is being renewed in knowledge after the image of its creator." Also see Ephesians 4:22.

        …**MEMORY VERSE**: Galatians 5:16 – "But I say, walk by the Spirit, and you will not carry out the desire of the flesh." If you walk by the Spirit there will be no need to rely on yourself!

        > **TEACHER'S NOTE:**
        > Walking by the Spirit implies both direction and empowerment – that is making decisions and choices according to the Holy Spirit's guidance, and acting with the spiritual power that the Spirit supplies – ESV Study Bible

    - Replacing self-reliance by cultivating humility and godliness. What does this look like in our lives?

5. By planting humility and godliness, there is no room for self-reliance.

- Humility

    …What is humility? (Q #8) C. J. Mahaney's definition: "honestly assessing ourselves in the light of God's holiness and our sinfulness." Philippians 2:3 NIV – "Do nothing out of selfish ambition or vain conceit, but in humility consider others better than yourselves."

    …What is necessary to cultivate humility? A fresh view of the cross. (Q #9) Remind ourselves of 2 Corinthians 5:21 – "For our sake He made Him to be sin, who knew no sin, so that in Him we might become the righteousness of God." Isaiah 53:5 NASB – "He was pierced through for our transgressions."

    …When we look at the cross we see: 1) Jesus bearing our sin – exactly what we deserve from God for each sin we commit; 2) the One whose flesh was nailed to the cross should have been us; 3) The holiness and justice of God all at the same time. His wrath against sin as He punished the "sin bearer" in our place!

    …As we cultivate a sense of humility, there is no more room for pride that leads to the desire to be like God.

- Godliness

    …What is Godliness? (Q #10-11) Definition: "The attitude of regarding God in everything all the time." Someone who is "God-centered," "God-glorifying," "God-esteeming." (p. 143-144)

    …1 Corinthians 10:31 – "Do all to the glory of God." Every aspect of our life has the potential to glorify God! 1 Timothy 4:7b-8 – "…Train yourself for godliness…" Do we truly do everything to the glory of God?

    …What is the opposite of Godliness? Ungodliness or disregarding God. When we try to take all the credit for doing anything good in our lives, we are being prideful. Pride is rooted in ungodliness because we are totally disregarding God.

    …How do we fight for godliness? By seeing the cross as the overarching message and meaning of life. Discipline ourselves to practice the presence of God. 2 Corinthians 10:5 – "Take every thought captive to obey Christ." Philippians 4:8 – "Finally, brothers, whatever is true, whatever is noble, whatever is right, whatever is pure, whatever is lovely, whatever is admirable – if anything is excellent or praiseworthy – think about such things." Replace the lie with God's truth. If we're thinking about God at all times, there is no room for anything else!

A View of all Three Focal Points in 1 Corinthians 2:1-13

Paul was a great biblical example of someone who used all three focal points to shift his dependence back to the Power of the Holy Spirit. In his own life he:

#1 – Recognized his own weakness

#2 – Acknowledged the reliable power of the Holy Spirit

#3 – Rejected his own self reliance

By doing this, Paul was able to shift dependence off of himself and back to the Power of the Holy Spirit (the Second Bookend). 1 Corinthians 2:3-5 – "…my speech and my message were not in plausible words of wisdom, but in demonstration of the Spirit and of power that your faith might not rest in the wisdom of men but in the power of God."

After Preaching the Gospel to yourself everyday make a Daily Declaration of Dependence (Q #13)

1. I recognize my absolute lack of power and ability.

2. I redirect my dependence to the supremely reliable power of the Holy Spirit.

3. I reject my tendency to self-reliance: "You are God, and I am not."

TO SUM IT UP

"We work hard in the strength He provides, not to earn merit but to glorify and enjoy Him." (p. 146)

SONG

"Jesus Messiah" by Chris Tomlin

DISCUSSION TIME

1. Which one of the three focal points do you identify with the most that will help you lean more on the Power of the Holy Spirit?

2. How can the truths found in 1 Corinthians 15:10 and 2 Corinthians 4:7 encourage you in your dependence on the Bookends of the Christian life? (Q #14)

    - I Corinthians 15:10 – "By the grace of God I am what I am, and His grace toward me was not in vain. On the contrary, I worked harder than any one of them, though it was not I, but the grace of God that is with me."

    - 2 Corinthians 4:7 – "We have this treasure in jars of clay, to show that the surpassing power belongs to God and not to us. We are afflicted in every way, but not crushed; perplexed, but not driven to despair; persecuted, but not forsaken; struck down, but not destroyed…LEADER'S GUIDE

CONCLUSION

The Bookends Personal Worldview

What is a worldview? (Q #1)

1. An all-encompassing framework of ideas and beliefs through which an individual views and interacts with the world. (p. 149)
2. It provides a system for interpreting and applying knowledge and it affects how we view all of life and how we make decisions.

The Bookends offers a good "personal worldview" (Q #2)

1. A frame of reference that provides clarity and guidance for our day-to-day decision-making process and actions. (p. 150)
2. At any given time, all Christians are occupied in one or more of these three areas of sin:
    - Battling sin
    - Actively sinning
    - In the aftermath of sin

The Bookends worldview is helpful in all these areas (Q #3)

1. Battling sin
    - We must lean on the second bookend, the Power of the Holy Spirit, to provide the strength we need to be obedient and not give in to temptation.
    - We also must look at the Righteousness of Christ. Our gratitude for the Gospel motivates us to turn from our sin and return love to Him by obedience.
2. Actively sinning
- Whether it is self-righteousness, persistent guilt, or self-reliance, in all cases we haven't relied on the Righteousness of Christ and the Power of the Holy Spirit to receive grace and avoid sinning.
3. Aftermath of sin
    - We must renew our dependence on the first bookend by preaching the Gospel to ourselves every day! Remember Christ lived the life we should have lived, and died the death we should have died.
    - His obedience and death is all sufficient for reconciling us to God.
    - We rely on the Holy Spirit to reveal our sin, draw us to the cross, and enable our repentance and transformation.
4. Bookends worldview also helps with: (Q #4)
    - Interpersonal relationships: marriage, parenting, extended family, friends, coworkers, etc.

- Circumstances
- Decision making: regarding time, money, lifestyles
- Most importantly: motivations and dependencies

The Bookends worldview provides a constant awareness of these two fundamental realities: (Q #5)

1. We're 100% dependent on a righteousness and strength outside ourselves.
2. We remain 100% responsible for the placement of each of our books on the bookshelf of our lives.

The Bookends worldview is useful because it is the application of biblical doctrine and transforming truth that stabilizes our faith and sanctifies our lives!

Where do we go from here?

1. We are to be like the Prophet Isaiah who said, "Here am I! Send me!" from Isaiah 6:8. (Q #6) Respond to the Gospel with a gratitude so deep that it motivates us to be willing to be used by God however He chooses.
2. The Christian life is not only about our personal justification and sanctification. It's fulfilling the Great Commission.
    - Go out into the world, share the gospel, and make disciples.
    - Lives filled with "selfless serving, radical giving, and sacrificial living" (p. 154)

The impact of being covered by the perfect Righteousness of Christ and being enabled by the Power of the Holy Spirit should change everything. It did for me and I pray it does for you, too!

Jude 24-25 – "Now to Him who is able to keep you from stumbling and to present you blameless before the presence of His glory with great joy, to the only God, or Savior, through Jesus Christ our Lord, be glory, majesty, dominion, and authority, before all time and now and forever. Amen"

GOSPEL-PROCLAIMING SCRIPTURE

Romans 3:23 – All have sinned and fall short of the glory of God.

1 Peter 1:15-16 – But he who called you is holy; you also be holy in all your conduct.

Romans 3:10 – None is righteous, no not one.

Isaiah 64:6 – …all our righteous deeds are like a polluted garment.

Galatians 3:10 – Cursed by everyone who does not abide by all things written in the book of the Law and do them.

Romans 6:23 – For the wages of sin is death, but the gift of God is eternal life in Christ Jesus our Lord.

Galatians 3:13 – Christ redeemed us from the curse of the law by becoming a curse for us.

1 Peter 2:24 – He bore our sin in His body on the tree.

Romans 5:8 – But God demonstrates his own love for us in this: while we were still sinners, Christ died for us.

1 Peter 3:18 – For Christ also suffered once for sins, the righteous for the unrighteous.

Romans 6:23b – …but the gift of God is eternal life in Christ Jesus.

2 Corinthians 5:21 – For our sake he made him to be sin who knew no sin, so that in him we might become the righteousness of God.

Isaiah 61:10 – …for he has clothed me with the garments of salvation and he has covered me with the robe of righteousness.

In Christ Alone
By Owl City

In Christ alone my hope is found,
He is my light, my strength, my song;
this Cornerstone, this solid Ground,
firm through the fiercest drought and storm.
What heights of love, what depths of peace,
when fears are stilled, when strivings cease!
My Comforter, my All in All,
here in the love of Christ I stand.

There in the ground His body lay
Light of the world by darkness slain:
Then bursting forth in glorious Day
Up from the grave he rose again!
And as He stands in victory
Sin's curse has lost its grip on me,
For I am His and He is mine –
Bought with the precious blood of Christ.

No guilt in life, no fear in death,
This is the power of Christ in me;
From life's first cry to final breath.
Jesus commands my destiny.
No power of hell, no scheme of man,
Can ever pluck me from His hand;
Till He returns or calls me home,
Here in the power of Christ I'll stand.

Till He returns or calls me home,
Here in power of Christ I'll stand.
Here in the power of Christ I'll stand.

Motion Of Mercy
By Francesca Battistelli

I was poor I was weak
I was the definition of the spiritually
Bankrupt condition
So in need of help

I was unsatisfied
Hungry and thirsty
When You rushed to my side
So unworthy
Still You gave yourself away…

[Chorus]
That's the motion of mercy
Changing the way and the why we are
That's the motion of mercy
Moving my heart

Now I'm filled by a love
That calls me to action
I was empty before now I'm drawn to compassion
And to give myself away

[Chorus]
That's the motion of mercy
Changing the way and the why we are
That's the motion of mercy
Moving my heart

Living for the lost
Loving 'til it hurts
No matter what the cost
Like You loved me first
That's the motion of mercy

God give me strength to give something for nothing
I wanna be a glimpse of the Kingdom that's coming soon

[Chorus]
That's the motion of mercy
Changing the way and the why we are
That's the motion of mercy
Moving my heart

The Solid Rock
By Avalon

My hope is built on nothing less
Than Jesus' blood and righteousness
I dare not trust the sweetest frame
But wholly lean on Jesus' name

(I'm leanin' on Jesus)
(I'm leanin' on Jesus, Jesus)
(I'm leanin' on You)

When darkness fails, His lovely face
I rest on His unchanging grace
(Every high and stormy gale)
In every high and stormy gale
(My anchor holds within the veil)
My anchor holds within the veil

On Christ, the solid rock, I stand
All other ground is sinking sand
All other ground is sinking sand
(All other ground is sinking, sinking)
(All other ground is sinking, sinking sand)

His oath, His covenant, His blood
Support me in the whelming flood
When all around my soul gives way
He then is all my Hope and Stay
On Christ, the solid rock, I stand
All other ground is sinking sand
All other ground is sinking sand
A sign of love

When He shall come with trumpet sound
Oh, may I then, in Him be found
Dressed in His righteousness, alone
Faultless to stand before the throne

On Christ, the solid rock, I stand
All other ground is sinking sand
All other ground is sinking sand

On Christ, the solid rock, I stand
All other ground is sinking sand
All other ground is sinking sand

All other ground is sinking sand
All other ground is sinking sand
No other, I'm leanin' on Jesus
All other ground is sinking sand

Hold me in, I'm leanin' on Jesus
All other ground is sinking sand
'Cause on a rock, I stand

Not Guilty
By Mandisa

I stand accused
There's a list a mile long
Of all my sins
Of everything that I've done wrong
I'm so ashamed
There's nowhere left for me to hide
This is the day
I must answer for my life

My fate is in the Judge's hands
But then He turns to me and says

I know you
I love you
I gave My life to save you
Love paid the price for mercy
My verdict not guilty

How can it be?
I can't begin to comprehend
What kind of grace
Would take the place of all my sin?

I stand in awe
Now that I have been set free
And the tears well up as I look at that cross
'Cause it should have been me

My fate was in the nail-scarred hands
He stretched them out for me and said

[Chorus]

I'm falling on my knees to thank You
With everything I am I'll praise You
So grateful for the words I heard You say

[Chorus]

Grace
By Laura Story

My heart is so proud, my eyes are so unfocused.
I see the things You do through me as great things I have done.
And now You gently break me, then lovingly You take me
And hold me as my Father and mold me as my Maker.

I ask You: "How many times will You pick me up,
When I keep on letting You down?
And each time I will fall short of Your glory,
How far will forgiveness abound?"
And You answer: "My child, I love you.
And as long as you're seeking My face,
You'll walk in the power of My daily sufficient grace."

At times I may grow weak and feel a bit discouraged,
Knowing that someone, somewhere could do a better job.
For who am I to serve You? I know I don't deserve You.
And that's the part that burns in my heart and keeps me hanging on.

I ask You: "How many times will You pick me up,
When I keep on letting You down?
And each time I will fall short of Your glory,
How far will forgiveness abound?"
And You answer: "My child, I love you.
And as long as you're seeking My face,
You'll walk in the power of My daily sufficient grace."

You are so patient with me, Lord.

I ask You: "How many times will You pick me up,
When I keep on letting You down?
And each time I will fall short of Your glory,
How far will forgiveness abound?"
And You answer: "My child, I love you.
And as long as you're seeking My face,
You'll walk in the power of My daily sufficient grace."

In Me
By Casting Crowns

If you ask me to leap
Out of my boat on the crashing waves
If You ask me to go
Preach to the lost world that Jesus saves

I'll go, but I cannot go alone
Cause I know I'm nothing on my own
But the power of Christ in me makes me strong
Makes me strong

Cause when I'm weak, You make me strong
When I'm blind, You shine Your light on me
Cause I'll never get by living on my own ability
How refreshing to know You don't need me
How amazing to find that you want me
So I'll stand on Your truth, and I'll fight with Your strength
Until You bring the victory, by the power of Christ in me

If You ask me to run
And carry Your light into foreign land
If You ask me to fight
Deliver Your people from Satan's hand

To reach out with Your hands
To learn through Your eyes
To love with the love of a savior
To feel with Your heart
And to think with Your mind
I'd give my last breath for Your glory

I Will Abide
By Christ For the Nations and Lauren Farmer

I will abide under the shadow of Your wings
In the shelter of Your arms I will be
And I will trust in You Your hand is leading me
My soul will follow hard after Thee

[Chorus]
The mercies of Your heart awaken the dawn
In You my joy is found complete
Undone have I become humbled by You
You're everything I long to be

[BRIDGE]
Jesus Savior God of mine
You alone have ransomed my life
King forever Redeemer and Friend
I belong to You my Beloved

Strong Enough
By Matthew West

You must
You must think I'm strong
To give me what I'm going through

Well, forgive me
Forgive me if I'm wrong
But this looks like more than I can do
On my own

[Chorus]
I know I'm not strong enough to be
Everything that I'm supposed to be
I give up
I'm not strong enough
Hands of mercy won't you cover me
Lord right now I'm asking you to be
Strong enough
Strong enough
For the both of us

Well, maybe
Maybe that's the point
To reach the point of giving up

Cause when I'm finally
Finally at rock bottom
Well, that's when I start looking up
And reaching out

[Chorus]

Cause I'm broken
Down to nothing
But I'm still holding on to the one thing
You are God
And you are strong
When I am weak

I can do all things
Through Christ who gives me strength
And I don't have to be
Strong enough
Strong enough
(Repeat)

Oh, yeah

[Chorus]

Holy Spirit Have Your Way
By Leeland

Long after the tears fall I'm still your child
I put down my defenses and lay down my pride
Love and forgiveness flow in deep and wide
So I run to you and surrender all!

As I lay down my life
And pick up my cross
What a joy it is to give my life away to you
All that I need,
All that I seek
Is You here with me
Holy Spirit have Your way in me!

In times of trouble, though trials may come
The rock of ages is standing strong
I'm fighting battles, but the war is won
So I'll run to you and surrender all

As I lay down my life
And pick up my cross
What a joy it is to give my life away to you
All that I need,
All that I seek
Is You here with me
Holy Spirit have Your way in me!

More of You and less of me, God
More of You and less of me, God
More of You and less of me, God
More of You overflowing

As I lay down my life
And pick up my cross
What a joy it is to give my life away to you
All that I need,
All that I seek
Is You here with me
Holy Spirit have Your way in me!
Holy Spirit have Your way in me!

Jesus Messiah
By Chris Tomlin

He became sin, who knew no sin
That we might become His righteousness
He humbled himself and carried the cross

Love so amazing, love so amazing

Jesus Messiah, name above all names
Blessed redeemer, Emmanuel
The rescue for sinners, the ransom from Heaven
Jesus Messiah, Lord of all

His body the bread, his blood the wine
Broken and poured out all for love
The whole earth trembled, and the veil was torn

Love so amazing, love so amazing, yeah

Jesus Messiah, name above all names
Blessed redeemer, Emmanuel
The rescue for sinners, the ransom from Heaven
Jesus Messiah, Lord of all

All I hope is in You, all I hope is in You
All the glory to You, God, the light of the world

Jesus Messiah, name above all names
Blessed redeemer, Emmanuel
The rescue for sinners, the ransom from Heaven
Jesus Messiah, Lord of all

Thomas Wilcox's instructions for dealing with persistent guilt:

Shift your focus Away from your sin and onto Christ

1. As Paul did, 1 Timothy 1:13-14 – "Formerly I was a blasphemer, persecutor..."<u>But</u> I received mercy... and the grace of our Lord overflowed for me ... Christ Jesus came into the world to save sinners of whom I am the foremost."

2. Paul recognized his sin...but he didn't stay there. He turned to the Gospel.

3. **Guilt-Conviction-Gospel-Repentance**

    - Don't wallow in your guilt! Take it to the cross and leave it there.
    - Then turn away from your sin. Ezekiel 18:30b – "Repent and turn from all your transgressions."
    - This is only possible with the power of the Holy Spirit.

Shift your focus to Christ our Mediator

1. Hebrews 9:15 "Therefore, he is the **mediator** of a new covenant, so that those who are called may receive that promised eternal inheritance..."

    - Christ is our High Priest who offered Himself as the perfect sacrifice!

2. Hebrews 4:14,16 – "We have a great high priest...let us then with confidence draw near to the throne of grace, that we may receive mercy and find grace to help in time of need.

    - Since Christ paid our debt, remember we are clothed with His righteousness and we can have a relationship with Him and approach Him with confidence!

3. Hebrews 10:19 – "Since we have confidence to enter the holy places by the blood of Jesus, but the new and living way that he opened for us through the curtain, that is, through his flesh."

Shift your focus to Christ crucified, risen, and ascended

1. Mark 16:5-6 – "Jesus was crucified and risen."

2. Luke 24:51 – Jesus' ascension – "He was carried into heaven."

3. I Corinthians 15:3-4 – "Christ died, was buried and was raised on the third day."

    - Christ is not still on the cross! He rose again and conquered sin and death!

4. Galatians 2:20 – "I have been crucified with Christ. It is no longer I who live, but Christ who lives in me."

    - Remember what His crucifixion means for us! We have been redeemed and are free to live in Christ.

5. Ephesians 1:20-21 – Christ is "seated at the right hand in the heavenly places, far above all rule and authority..."

    - He is seated in the heavens as our advocate and our mediator, which leads us to...

Shift your focus to the glory of Christ

1. Colassians 3:1 – "If then you have been raised with Christ, seek the things that are above, where Christ is, seated at the right hand of God. Set your minds on things that are above, not on things that are on earth."

2. Hebrews 8:1 – "We have such a high priest, who is seated at the right throne of the Majesty in heaven."

3. Let's remember who this is about…as high and lifted up as He is…

    - Isaiah 43:25 – "I, am he, who blots our your transgressions for my own sake, I will not remember your sins."
    - 1 John 2:12 – "your sins are forgiven for his name's sake."
    - Ezekiel 36:22 – "It is not for your sake." It's not about us!
    - God saved us because He loves us but not necessarily for our sake, but to demonstrate His grace which ultimately gives Him glory!

Shift your focus off of self-condemnation

1. Romans 8:1 – "There is therefore now no condemnation for those who are in Christ Jesus."
2. If we declare ourselves guilty it neglects the Gospel message of grace, forgiveness, and hope!

Shift your focus of self-contempt

- If were wallowing in our guilt, we need to realize that we are focused on ourselves! It is a form of self-centeredness, which is the opposite of Christ-centeredness. Shift our focus back onto Christ!

A View of All Three Focal Points for Shifting our Dependence to the Second Bookend
Demonstrated in the Life of Paul (1 Corinthians 2:1-13)

Use as reference: The Three Focal Points are:

#1 – Our Desperate Weakness

#2 – The Reliable Power of the Holy Spirit

#3 – Rejection of Self-Reliance.

I Corinthians 2:1-2 – "I did not come proclaiming to you the testimony of God with lofty speech or wisdom. For *I decided to know nothing among you* except Jesus Christ and Him crucified."

- Even though Paul was very intelligent and probably knew his scripture inside out, he made it clear that he was *not relying on his own wisdom.* Focal point #3

- He *acknowledged his own weakness* and pointed straight to the gospel. Focal point #1

Verses 3-5 – "…my *speech and my message were not in plausible words of wisdom,* (focal point #3) but in demonstration of the Spirit and of power that your faith might *not rest in the wisdom of men* but in the power of God."

- He pointed that his message was *only by the power of the Holy Spirit.*

- He wanted others *not* to rely on Paul's wisdom but on the power of God. Focal point #2

Verse 7 – "We impart a secret and hidden wisdom of God, which God decreed before the ages of our glory…"

- Paul points us to the *wisdom of God* that was "before the foundation of the world." (Ephesians 1:4) Focal point #2

Verse 9 – "What no eye has seen, nor ear heard, nor the heart of man imagined, what God has prepared for those who love Him."

- A wisdom that goes *beyond our imagination* of what He planned for us.

- Quoted from Isaiah 64:4 "From old no one has heard or perceived by the ear, no eye has seen a God besides you, who acts for those who wait for Him." We wait with anticipation and express dependence on *what He has planned for us.* (Focal point #2)

Verse 10, 12-13 – "These things God has revealed to us through the Spirit. For the Spirit searches everything, even the depths of God. Now we have received…the Spirit who is from God, that we might understand the things freely given us by God. And we impart this in words *not taught by human wisdom* (Focal point #3) but *taught by the spirit*, interpreting spiritual truths to those who are spiritual." (Focal point #2)

- Paul is emphasizing that it is *only the Power of the Holy Spirit that reveals to us God's truth!* Therefore Paul is revealing his dependence on the Holy Spirit.

THE BOOKENDS OF THE CHRISTIAN LIFE

BOOK BY JERRY BRIDGES & BOB BEVINGTON

BIBLE STUDY

CHAPTER ONE
First Bookend: The Righteousness of Christ

1. What does the Bible mean by the word *"righteous"*? (page 19)

2. Read Matthew 22:36-40 and 1 Peter 1:15-16. What is God's standard for the level of righteousness He requires of us? Why? (20)

3. Read Romans 3:10 and Isaiah 64:6. What does God's Word say about our righteousness?

4. Read Galatians 3:10-13.

    - What happens when we are unable to "abide by all things?" (20)

    - What did Christ do for us?

5. What is the difference between trusting in Christ for our eternal destiny versus trusting Him for our *day-to-day* standing with God? (21)

6. Read 2 Corinthians 5:21. In light of 2 Corinthians 5:21, read 1 Peter 2:22 and Hebrews 4:15. What does God's Word say about Jesus' level of obedience here on this earth? (22)

- 2 Corinthians 5:21 says that God "made Jesus to be sin." According to 1 Peter 2:24, how did Jesus do this? (24)

- Read Matthew 27:46. Explain the significance of the first sentence on page 24 of the book, "The physical pain He endured was nothing compared to the agony of being separated from the Father." What does this say about Jesus' relationship with His father at the time of Jesus' death?

  How does Jesus' relationship with the Father being broken result in ours being restored?

- 2 Corinthians 5:21 says "so that in him we might become the righteousness of God." At the moment we put our faith in what Christ did for us on the cross, according to Isaiah 61:10, what happens?

  How are we presented before our God? When He looks at us, who does He see?

- As a result of this "Great Exchange," according to Romans 5:1, "By faith" we are _____.

7. Explain the connection between Christ's righteousness and our justification. (26)

8. Faith involves both a *renunciation* and a *reliance*.

- In terms of the first bookend, what kind of renunciation is required of us? (28)

- Where must we place our reliance? Be specific.

9. What does it look like when we stand in the present reality of our justification every day? What difference will it make in our day-to-day, moment-to-moment lives? (27-30)

10. The final paragraph on page 30 asks several questions. Try to answer them based on what you have read in chapter one.

CHAPTER TWO
The Motivation of the Gospel

1. Read Luke 7:36-50.

    - In the story of the sinful woman, why is Simon the Pharisee upset?

    - There is a profound difference between the way Simon and the woman treated Jesus. What does this tell us about how they viewed their sinfulness? (page 31-33)

    - Thinking back on your last several months, has your attitude toward your sin been more like Simon or the woman? Why?

2. None of us loves Christ the way He deserves to be loved. Genuine love for Christ comes through two important understandings. What are they? (34)

3. How does the story of the sinful woman depict the truth of the first paragraph on page 35? How can you apply this to yourself?

4. Read Isaiah 6:1-5.

    - How does Isaiah respond to seeing the Lord?

- How does he view himself in light of being in the presence of a Holy God? (35)

5. Put yourself in Isaiah's place. Do you think you would have responded the way Isaiah did in verse 5? Why or why not?

6. How was Isaiah's experience similar to that of the sinful woman of Luke 7? What were the three common steps? (36)

7. In light of these three steps, what can you do to grow in your experience of the motivating power of the Gospel?

8. Read Philippians 3:4-9.

    - According to verse 6, *if* Paul's righteousness was based on following the law, what would he be considered?

    - According to verses 7-9, where does Paul realize his righteousness *actually* comes from?

9. Read Philippians 3:7-14. Paul renounced his own righteousness and relied solely on the righteousness of Christ. How did that fuel his desire to pursue Christ-likeness and serve God whole-heartedly? (38)

10. Read Romans 12:1. In light of the Gospel message of mercy, how are we to present our bodies?

    - Explain the significance of the expression a *living sacrifice*. (39)

11. Consider making an application for your life based on Romans 12:1.

CHAPTER THREE
Gospel Enemy #1: Self-Righteousness

1. Describe in your own words what it means to be self-righteous.

2. What is the difference between self-righteousness *toward God* and self-righteousness *toward others*? Which is worse, and why? (page 41-42)

3. Read Galatians 2:21. How does the belief that we have earned (merited) God's blessings "nullify grace" and set us up for committing self-righteousness toward God? (42-43)

4. Read Galatians 1:6-9.

    - Why was Paul "astonished" with the Galatians?

    - Explain in your own words what Paul meant by a *different gospel*?

5. Read Galatians 2:16 and fill in the blanks. "Yet we know that a person is not justified by _____, but through _____ in _____."

    - In Chapter One we discussed that being justified means we are declared righteous (in right standing) with God. According to Galatians 2:16, how are we justified?

- Are we justified (declared righteous) by our own works?

6. The second paragraph on page 44 describes the basis most people give for their belief that God will accept them into heaven.

    - Why is this approach considered to be *self-righteous*?

    - Read Matthew 7:21-23. What does Jesus indicate His response will be to this large group of people who base their acceptance from God on their own works?

7. Many people bank on the hope that God will consider their good deeds to have enough redeeming value to offset the guilt of their bad deeds. Why is this a dangerous assumption? (45)

8. Think about your recent prayer times. Are you confident in your underlying assumptions and attitudes about why God should favorably answer your prayers?

9. Isaiah 64:6 says that all of our righteous deeds are like _____. Now read Luke 18:9-14.

    - Why was this Pharisee thankful that he was not like the "other men?"

- On what was the Pharisee basing his righteousness?

- On what was the tax collector basing his appeal to God?

- According to Jesus (verse 14) why was the tax collector justified, rather than the Pharisee?

10. Describe the self-righteous moralistic believer. (47-49) Based on your answers to the ten questions on page 49, do you tend to fit in this category?

11. Why is persistent guilt actually a form of self-righteousness toward God? (50-51)

12. Do you agree that most believers vacillate between moralistic, performance-based self-righteousness on one hand, and persistent guilt on the other? Which category do you lean toward more, and why? (50-51)

13. Explain the last sentence on page 51.

14. From everything you've read in chapters 1-3, how does leaning on the First Bookend slay Gospel Enemy #1?

CHAPTER FOUR
Gospel Enemy #2: Persistent Guilt

1. Explain how those who embrace persistent guilt lean on the same object of dependency as those who embrace self-righteousness. (page 53)

2. Read Genesis 3:1-13. After Adam and Eve ate from the tree of knowledge of good and evil, what do you think it means that "the eyes of both were opened?"

3. What is a *conscience*? Explain in your own words.

   - What did God design the conscience to do for us?

   - What are its two purposes? (54)

4. Why do we tend to use different escape mechanisms when dealing with a guilty conscience? What is the purpose of these escape mechanisms? (55)

5. What have you used in the past to attempt to escape the voice of your conscience? Is this sinful? Why or why not? (55)

6. Describe how persistent guilt gets a stranglehold on believers. (55-56)

7. Read 1 Timothy 1:19. What can happen to our faith when we repeatedly reject our conscience?

8. How have the ten questions on pages 56 and 57 revealed the presence of persistent guilt in your life?

9. The idea that we must "forgive ourselves" has no basis in Scripture. Why do you think this concept has become so popular – even among Christians? (57)

10. Read Hebrews 9:14. What purifies our conscience?

11. Describe how the first bookend is the only way to defeat persistent guilt. (57-58)

12. Read 1 Timothy 1:13-14. Explain how a healthy remembrance of our sin can be a blessing. (58-59)

13. Puritan Thomas Wilcox described six ways to deal with persistent guilt by shifting our focus. Which of these do you find helpful and why? (59-61)

14. Describe how persistent guilt can be transformed into joyful gratitude for the gospel. (61-63)

CHAPTER FIVE
Leaning on the First Bookend

1. Explain what it means to "lean" on the First Bookend. (page 65)

2. Our unchangeable, infallible God provides the bookends – therefore they never move or fail. The problem is our failure to lean our books on them. Describe how this happens. How can we correct this? (65-66)

3. What are the three *focal points* for dependence-shifting?

4. Ephesians 1:18 speaks of "having the eyes of your hearts enlightened." What does it mean to "see" with the eyes of your heart, and why is this so important? (66)

5. Read Luke 19:1-10. Despite the crowd's disapproval of Zacchaeus, how does Zacchaeus respond to being in the presence of Jesus? (verse 8)

    - Why do you think Zacchaeus responded in this way?

    - Read verse 10 again and complete: "For the Son of Man came to seek and to save the _____."

- Was Zacchaeus saved because of his own righteousness?

6. Why is it vital that we see ourselves as desperately lost sinners?

7. See Psalm 36:9 and John 8:12. Explain in your own words what the author means when he says on page 68, "When we step into the light of Christ's perfect righteousness, our utter depravity is exposed"?

8. In what ways does reviewing the list on page 68 help you "see" yourself as a desperately lost sinner (Focal Point #1)? What happens to our dependence? (68-69)

9. Read the paragraph that starts on the bottom of page 69 and describe why the righteousness of Christ is all-sufficient for the needs of sinners.

10. It is not enough to merely see the righteousness of Christ as all-sufficient; we must see it as all-sufficient *for us*. Think about specific areas you desperately need the righteousness of Christ to substitute for your sin and failure. Is His righteousness sufficient for even *that*? How does this realization make you feel toward Him?

11. What does it mean to *preach the Gospel to yourself every day* and why is it so vital to your spiritual health? (70-72)

12. Read John 8:12. Explain why functional saviors could be described as evil. (72-74)

13. From the fill-in-the-blank exercise on page 73, identify your functional savior(s).

- Once we have identified our functional savior(s), what are we to do with them? What can happen when we don't reject our functional saviors? (74)

- Currently, what is God doing in your life to help free you from your functional savior(s)? (74)

CHAPTER SIX
Second Bookend: The Power of the Holy Spirit

1. Explain the difference between motivation and ability/power when it comes to living a Christian life. (page 81)

2. According to Ephesians 1:13, when are we sealed with the Holy Spirit?

3. In 2 Timothy 2:1 Paul wrote, "Be strengthened by the grace that is in Christ Jesus." Explain what it means to *"be strengthened."* (82)

4. Explain the difference in the two categories of grace: the blessing of privilege and the blessing of power. (82-83)

5. Read 2 Corinthians 12:9. Explain what this verse means in your own words.

6. Explain the difference between *help* and *enablement*. (85)

7. When discussing the role of our faith in leaning on the First Bookend, the authors state that faith involves both renunciation and reliance. Explain how these two terms apply to our role in leaning on the Second Bookend. (85)

8. From the section titled, The Sovereignty of the Holy Spirit, explain what the Holy Spirit being "sovereign" means. (85-86)

9. Why is it that when we rely on the Power of the Holy Spirit, sometimes He temporarily withholds His power while other times He dramatically manifests His power in us? (86)

10. From the section titled, "The Spirit's Synergistic Work" explain what is meant by the expression, "qualified synergism." Describe how this relieves us from the burden of having insufficient willpower and strength to obey God. (86-88)

11. Read 1 Peter 4:10-11 and Philippians 2:12-13. Explain how these passages are examples of qualified synergism.

12. In what ways is the Spirit's work "monergistic"? How have you experienced this in your life? (88-90)

13. What three words does the Heidelberg Catechism use in understanding the monergistic work of the Spirit? What do these words refer to? (89)

14. Describe the *similarities* and the *differences* between the first and second Bookends. (92)

CHAPTER SEVEN
Gospel Enemy #2: Persistent Guilt

1. Explain the concept of dependent responsibility from Colossians 1:29. (page 95-96)

2. Explain the two sentences that start on the bottom of page 98: "There's no conflict between our work and our dependence. In fact, the harder we work, the more absolute our dependence on the Spirit must become."

3. What is meant by the term "spiritual disciplines"? How do they benefit us? (99)

4. What two truths must we constantly keep in mind as we practice the spiritual disciplines? Why are these two truths so important? (99-100)

5. Explain how reading the Bible can become "a conversation, a process of talking to God and listening to Him" in an experience of daily fellowship with Him. (100)

6. Read 2 Corinthians 3:18. Explain in your own words what it means to "behold the glory of the Lord." How does this result in transformation?

7. What is involved in "preaching the gospel to yourself every day?" Why is this so important to your daily communion with God? (101)

8. Read Colossians 1:9-10 and Romans 12:2. Why is Scripture so instrumental in renewing and transforming our lives? What are some practical ways we can apply this truth to our daily lives? (102-103)

9. Explain in your own words how prayer is an expression of our dependency? How does prayer cause our dependency to grow? (103)

10. Read Romans 8:28-29. How does God use the circumstances in our lives (both good and "bad") as a means of grace in our lives? (104)

11. Read 1 Corinthians 1:9 and 1 John 1:3. What are we called to have with the Lord? In light of this, explain the differences between our union with Christ and our *communion* with Christ. (106)

12. Read Psalm 63:1 and Psalm 42:1-2. The Psalmists' vivid desire for communion with God is evident in these passages. From all you have read in *The Bookends* so far, what is there about God that would make Him *this* desirable to you?

13. What can you do to improve the quality of your daily communion with the Lord?

14. Who will give you the strength to carry out these desires?

CHAPTER EIGHT
The Help of the Divine Encourager

1. Why is the Holy Spirit referred to as the *Divine Encourager*? (page 109)

2. Read Galatians 5:5. Where does the Holy Spirit often point us for encouragement? (109-110)

3. Read John 14:26 and 15:26. In your own words, explain what Jesus meant when He said "The Helper…will bear witness about me."

4. What is *gratitude for purchased grace*? Why is it *life-changing*? (110-111)

5. Read 2 Corinthians 5:14-15 and 1 John 4:9-10,19. Explain what Paul meant when he said, "the love of Christ controls us."

6. Read the quote from Thomas Chalmers on page 113. Explain what it means to "replace the object of our sinful affection with an infinitely more worthy one-God himself."

7. Explain the difference between the diagrams on pages 113 and 114.

8. Think carefully about your life and then fill in the blank on page 115. Now read the paragraph that follows the blank and describe how you feel about God and your sin.

9. In your own words, describe what it means to enjoy your relationship with God? (116-117)

10. Read John 17:22-23. What remarkable statement does Jesus make about the impact of the Gospel on those who believe in Him?

11. How does a desire to enjoy your relationship with God empower your battle against sin? (118)

12. From the paragraph that starts at the bottom of page 118, describe how the Spirit uses the promises of God to equip us for our battle against sin.

13. From the paragraph that starts at the bottom of page 119, what spiritual disciplines can you commit to in order to prepare yourself for your future needs?

14. What are some of the promises from God's Word that the Spirit has used to motivate or encourage you in your walk?

CHAPTER NINE
Gospel Enemy #3: Self-Reliance

1. Why does it seem strange to think of self-reliance and its "cousins" as enemies of the Gospel? (page 123-124)

2. What is self-reliance? How does it compare to self-righteousness? (124)

3. According to John 15:5, what is wrong with a self-reliant approach to life? (125-126)

4. According to 1 Corinthians 4:7, why do you believe the authors state that we should not be self-reliant about *anything*? Do you agree? Why or why not?

5. The last paragraph on page 126 states that *all* believers are inclined to fall prey to self-reliance *every day*! Do you agree? What have you done in the last 24 hours that has not been done with 100% dependence on the power of the Holy Spirit?

6. Read Matthew 26:31-35. What was the object of Peter's dependence? In what ways do *our* acts of self-reliance resemble Peter's denial of Christ? (127-128)

7. Read Philippians 4:13 and 2 Corinthians 3:5-6. When we fall into a pattern of self-reliance, how can the truth from these scriptures shift our dependence back on the power of the Holy Spirit?

8. Read the story of Brian's struggle with self-reliance on pages 128-131. What similar patterns and outcomes have you seen in your own life?

9. Which of the four excerpts from John Newton do you identify with the most? Why? (131-132)

10. Read 2 Corinthians 12:7-8. What insights and applications do you find in the description of Paul's thorn in the flesh? (132-133) What types of "thorns" have you experienced?

11. Now read 2 Corinthians 12:9-10. How did this promise help Paul deal with his thorn in the flesh? Why do you suppose Paul was able to "boast" of and be "content" with his weaknesses?

12. What "thorn" can you be content with in your life?

13. In your own words, explain what Paul meant when he said, "For when I am weak, then I am strong?"

14. How can 2 Corinthians 12:9-10 help free you from self-reliance?

CHAPTER TEN
Leaning on the Second Bookend

1. The first paragraph in this chapter describes both bookends as "infinitely solid and weighty." Do you believe this? Why or why not? (page 135)

2. Read Isaiah 41:14-16. How does an earthworm accurately portray our weakness? What happens to transform us from "worm" to "threshing sledge"? (136-137)

3. Explain the term "progressive sanctification." How does it unfold in the life of the believer? Which comes first, justification or sanctification? (138)

4. Read 2 Corinthians 3:18.

    - Explain what the authors meant by saying "...the process of our transformation into Christ-likeness, involved 'seeing'?"

    - Using 2 Corinthians 3:18, complete this sentence. "For this comes from the _____ who is the _____. What is the power source of this transformation?

5. When we place our dependency on the power of the Holy Spirit, it seems like sometimes He comes through for us, but sometimes He doesn't. How can you explain this apparent inconsistency? (139-140)

6. Spiritual warfare is a daily battle. How does the truth from 2 Corinthians 10:3-4 and Philippians 1:6 give you hope for these battles? (140)

7. Self-reliance is tenacious like poison ivy because its root system is extensive. Identify and describe the root of the Gospel enemies. (141-142)

8. What is humility? How does it address our self-reliance at its roots? (143)

9. Why is a "fresh view of the cross" needed in order to cultivate humility? (143)

10. What is godliness? How does it address our self-reliance at its roots? (143-144)

11. Read 1 Corinthians 10:31 and 2 Corinthians 10:5. How can we pursue godliness? (143-144)

12. Read 1 Corinthians 2:1-13. How are all three Focal Points for shifting our dependence on the second bookend demonstrated in this passage? (144-146)

13. Do you agree with the Daily Declaration of Dependence? (146)

14. How can the truths found in 1 Corinthians 15:10 and 2 Corinthians 4:7 encourage you in your dependence on the bookends of the Christian life?

CONCLUSION
The Bookends: A Personal Worldview

1. What is a "worldview" and why is it important? (page 149)

2. Explain how the Bookends can be a personal worldview. (149-150)

3. How is the Bookends Personal Worldview helpful in each of the three arenas of sin? (150-151)

4. Other than helping in our battle against sin, in what other areas does the Bookends Personal Worldview help? (152)

5. What does the Bookends Personal Worldview provide that makes it so helpful and worthwhile? (152-153)

6. How does Isaiah's response, "Here am I! Send me" reflect the ultimate goal of living between the Bookends? (153-154)

7. Read the second paragraph on page 154. Visualize the activities of your life from this moment forward as books that are stabilized and secured by leaning on both bookends. How does this change your outlook on life? How does it change your plans for the rest of the day, the rest of the week, and your long-term future?

8. Look back to the questions on page 16 and answer them again. How do your answers compare to those you wrote when you studied the Introduction?

- Summarize what you have learned from *The Bookends*.

Thanks for completing the Study Guide. If you have any comments or suggestions for the authors of **The Bookends of the Christian Life**, please submit them on the "Contact" page at TheBookendsBook.com.

Made in the USA
Las Vegas, NV
17 April 2023

70741385R00070